Financial Know-how for Non-financial Managers

Financial Know-how for Non-financial Managers

EASY WAYS TO UNDERSTAND ACCCOUNTS AND FINANCIAL PLANNING

John Spencer and Adrian Pruss

PIATKUS

First published in 1997 by
Judy Piatkus (Publishers) Ltd of
5 Windmill Street, London W1P 1HF

**The moral right of the authors
has been asserted**

A catalogue record for this book is
available from the British Library

ISBN 0 7499 1666 4

Edited by Elizabeth Hornby
Designed by Chris Warner
Illustrations by Chartwell Illustrators

Set by Action Typesetting Limited, Gloucester
Printed and bound in Great Britain by
Mackays of Chatham PLC

Contents

Foreword

---◇---

THERE is an ever-increasing trend, in large companies in particular, towards the devolution of responsibilities. In particular, the traditional area of budget-holding, for which some degree of accountancy or financial background or training was provided or demanded, is now being devolved at much lower levels. Along with this there is an increased emphasis on implementing simplified budgeting systems to allow non-financial people to hold budgets; and an increased demand for training of the kind reflected in this book, to enable companies to make their new budget-holders more financially aware.

All companies have come to understand the need to control cashflows and working capital if they are to develop in the short term. Managers at all levels are given very strict guidelines about what they can and cannot do, can and cannot spend, so that overall strategic planning is balanced. Those managers don't always feel that the reasons for those constraints are communicated to them, leaving them feeling unempowered in their own departments, and unable to explain to their subordinates why they seem to be imposing unnecessary difficulties. In fact mostly they *are* in receipt of the explanations, but they don't understand them: the information is given by the finance department in a way that does not communicate, and little of the explanation is understood. Non-financial managers read only the conclusions and not the detail because they are not trained to understand the detail. The manager reading this book will understand, in simple terms, how to read those statements, what other perti-

nent information to ask for, and how to further communicate them to others. In companies where such information is
not given – or where the finance department has given up
sending out the information because no one understood it
anyway – this book will fill in the missing blanks.

The book contains several chapters, such as *Accounting
Ratios and How to Use Them*, which allow for analysis of
presented figures. As long as the financial information flow
is in the hands of the finance departments, many managers
are powerless to get to understand anything not presented to
them on that plate. By being able to read behind the figures,
they can find out facts they want to know, and then be able
to ask the finance department for the more relevant information for their department. In short, managers get the
information they want, not what is fed to them.

Long-term views and needs are well catered for in this
book. Capital expenditure budgeting, fixed asset policies,
and the application of depreciation are all explained in
simple terms that allow the manager to take a more-than-
year view of his or her department. It allows also for valuable
input to the longer-term strategic planning and ensures that
neither the manager nor the department is sidelined by those
with finance backgrounds getting 'the biggest slice of the
cake'.

Of course, the budget is where the manager usually faces
the finance department head-to-head on a daily basis. This
book approaches the ethos of budgeting, and the practical-
ities of it, very effectively. Not only does it explain how to
deal with the numbers, but how to deal with the people: how
to use the budget to motivate instead of just to measure, how
to use it to plan rather than just monitor. There are several
chapters which go hand-in-hand with this: *Cost-Cutting
Exercises*, for example, offers practical steps to take when
the budget variances are working against you.

This book provides the manager with many ways to make
the finance department see things the manager's way, or
forces accountants to answer questions raised in plain
English, to the manager's benefit. But when you can't beat

them, and you have to join them, the book provides a useful glossary – *Parlez-vous Accountancy?* – breaking into the language of the accountant.

John Spencer and Adrian Pruss are at the forefront of this training and conduct regular training sessions for our merchant bank. Their several decades of combined experience has been gained from developing and implementing significant change programmes within large and multi-national companies, many of which have also now adopted these new approaches to budget-holding. Having been involved in the initial change programmes and having instigated new and radical corporate structures in such a range of organisations, they are extremely well qualified to design the support structures for these new systems. As trainers of many years' experience they have the added advantage of being able to deliver the necessary training. This book is therefore the combination of their many years' focus on finance for non-financial managers, and arrives on the bookshelves at the precise time when companies are crying out for just this information, presented in just this way: crisp, concise and relevant.

Paul Hartwell
Director
West Merchant

Introduction

————◇————

AFTER TEN YEARS as an engineer on oil tankers sailing around the world, Tony decided it was time to take a desk job on land. He was appointed training manager of the engineering section of a major oil refining company; his brief was to run the technical training programmes. For several years he was content in his job; he knew the subject, knew the people, and knew the company. He could relate to their challenges; after all, he'd been on the tankers where they were now. When they had a problem he could deal with it; he'd held the same spanners in his hand, got his hands dirty, and he spoke their language.

Two years ago he became a very unhappy man. His job had changed, and he couldn't understand the changes. The company expanded his role without explanation or training; now they seemed to want him to be a financial manager as well. They were giving him responsibility and control of his budget, they were asking him to justify his revenue and capital expenditure requirements, and they wanted him to deal directly with the accounts department who, in his view, were just a bunch of bean-counters.

Frankly, he had even thought about taking early retirement.

He decided to unburden himself to Mike, in Research and Development. Mike was young, adaptable, and presumably at ease with these new financial requirements. But when Tony spoke to Mike he found someone much like himself – except that the option of early retirement wasn't even on the horizon. Mike was a graduate chemist and at work he loved nothing more than to 'play with his chemistry set' as Tony and he had once joked. Now he had a budget too, and a need to talk to his colleagues and the accounts department in financial terms; and he was no more at ease with their jargon and concepts than was Tony.

So how did Tony, Mike, and a few hundred thousand other people in companies up and down the UK get into this position? And what can they do about it? This book is their solution.

This book started life as a training course for one client company – the one that Tony and Mike worked for. And in the past few years we have been called on to deliver tailored versions of this course to many other large PLCs in the UK.

The driving forces for the changes can be summarised as follows:

▶ **Legislation** With the financial fiascos that have featured in the press in recent years, there has been a move towards tighter controls. This has meant that directors have been made more accountable to their shareholders and creditors, and companies have been made more accountable to the public. Their response has had to be to push that responsibility downwards to all levels of management in the organisation.

▶ **Decentralisation of management** Large companies and groups of companies have disposed of huge accounting departments dealing with the whole overview and now expect each individual company or department to deal with their own administration, including finance. One of our clients – a multinational – has recently insisted that its UK subsidiary now, for the first time, deals with its own finances. In the subsidiary the response has been to push the accountability for budgets and financial decisions to the first-line manager level. Many organisations formerly in the public sector have been privatised, with much the same result. (And in our experience many of those companies had had even less exposure to finance and have found the change a frightening and overwhelming one.)

▶ **Integrated accounting systems** bringing together purchases, sales, production planning, staff planning and so on. Many large companies now have 'instant access, on-line', financial packages where every manager (sometimes without realising it) directly inputs to the system from their desktop PC. Management complained to us that the systems were being abused, almost crashed, by first-line managers inputting garbage to the system because they did not understand the system's requirements. Capital expenditure requests, for example, were 'half-baked' (to quote one senior manager); there was no understanding of payback periods, or cashflows.

▶ **Objectives** The current business trend is for the empowered manager to agree a clear set of objectives, which he or she must deliver within budget. The measure of success or failure is expressed as profitability and cashflow. Keeping your job now, more than ever, depends on your succeeding; and many managers are paid according to their performance, rather than a fixed annual salary.

The result of these changes is that many people who would not traditionally have been required to have any financial understanding are now being held responsible for financial matters. As one first-line manager put it to us: 'When I started here I was only expected to manage people, which I was good at. Now I'm told I've got no job if I can't manage a budget.'

Inevitably this has meant that such people, with no accountancy training, have been forcibly manoeuvred into positions where they are communicating through accountancy language and procedures, and they are often talking to accountants who are not always the best at recognising that theirs is a specialist jargon, and that, to many, accountancy is a frightening field, best avoided.

This book is therefore designed for Tony, Mike and the hundreds of thousands of other new non-financial managers; the managers of any number of years' experience who now find the need to understand – to be aware of – financial matters. It is not, in one sense, for financial managers, financial experts and financial directors, though they will find it useful as they must learn to bridge the financial communication gap 'from their end'.

Many managers are now being asked to make what amount to financial inputs to business decisions. You may be part of a team that, say, has to assess a would-be 'partner' firm with which your department or company is going to work for a joint project. Will that company be able to sustain the investment, or will it leave your company picking up the tab? Has that company got a good financial track record, or not? And so on. This book provides you with the ability to understand the concepts behind the answers to those questions, and even to recognise the questions that need to be asked in the first place.

Because the book is for the non-financial manager rather than the accountancy expert, we keep it basic. You will find very quickly, as you apply your newfound expertise, that the basic principles hold true for all sizes of companies, and you will soon find the relevance in your working environment.

▶ You may be new to budget-holding, and daunted by the prospect of having to plan and account for your department's finances. Chapter 15 sets out your challenges, and the framework of your solutions. But consider also chapter 12 on cost-cutting; there are Brownie points for proactively improving the efficiency of your department.

▶ You could be a project manager and presented with the challenges of capital expenditure (Capex) and Capex proposals, i.e. the planning of long-term asset usage. Chapter 22 is your guideline, but consider also chapter 21 which deals with the role of depreciation and asset replacement.

▶ You could be in the licensing department, needing to consider the company you are licensing to. See chapters 5 and 6 for the basic information given in the company's profit and loss account and its balance sheets, and chapter 8 which provides for a detailed look 'behind the figures'.

▶ The final chapter, *Parlez-vous Accountancy?*, is an A–Z of accounting terms. Each entry gives a short explanation and a reference to the page(s) where you will find the subject covered in more detail.

We expect every manager will find at least some of these chapters relevant at some time in their career; and probably most within months of reading this book. So welcome to the world and the language of finance. Good reading!

1

The Business System

---◇---

IN THE INTRODUCTION we mentioned the concerns of Tony, Mike and others that they were being drawn into the financial background of companies, often against their will. In our experience we have found that attempts to tell people only the bits of jargon and practice that they need for their specific job – to give them the 'need to know' rather than the 'nice to know' – leaves them with a foundation of sand. They still do not see the whole picture, which is demoralising and disempowering, and they still cannot fully communicate overall company strategy in financial terms. Certainly they find it difficult to talk to the finance departments.

This chapter is the overview needed by all non-financial managers, in basic terms, to allow them to see where the financial aspects of their department fit into the whole. It sets the scene for all the subsequent chapters of the book.

TO UNDERSTAND finance and financial language it is important to understand the world to which it relates. Businesses exist for many reasons, most commonly for the provision of goods and services to customers and to create wealth for the owners. This requires certain resources.

In economic terms, the major resources in the business system are land, materials, labour and capital (money). The type of business determines what mix of resources is necessary. For example, a farmer needs land to raise animals, grow crops, and so on, whereas a solicitor needs only an office to practise law. All organisations, whether in the public or private sector, need to make the best use of the resources at their disposal. In general terms this means getting the highest productivity for the expenditure on that resource.

Resources can be recorded in many ways: barrels of oil in an oilfield, numbers of vacant beds in a hospital ward, number of available staff-hours, the amount of money in a bank account, and so on. In order to measure and compare like with like, resources in the business system are given a monetary value, creating a common standard, and a common language. The accountant's role is to express resources in money values and to record incomings and outgoings so that management can monitor the progress – successful or otherwise – of the business. Monthly, quarterly, and annual comparisons are used to make strategic and tactical decisions regarding the business.

The business system model (Figure 1.1) shows the relationship between *sources* of funds and *use* of funds. Some of the terms used are explained in the *Parlez-vous Accountancy* section and will be expanded upon more fully in other chapters. Very generally, the purpose of the business system is to make profits. This allows the owners of the business (the shareholders) to obtain a return on their investment, and retain some profits in the business to replace assets, acquire new assets, perhaps allow the company to grow and expand, and generally finance the company's ongoing activity.

However, while all businesses produce goods and/or services, some organisations are not in business to make a profit – charities, for example. The receipts of money allow them to operate by giving services, money and/or goods to those whom they support.

SOURCES OF FUNDS

Although we look at sources of finance in more detail in chapter 17, this business system model shows that companies obtain money from a variety of sources – family and friends,

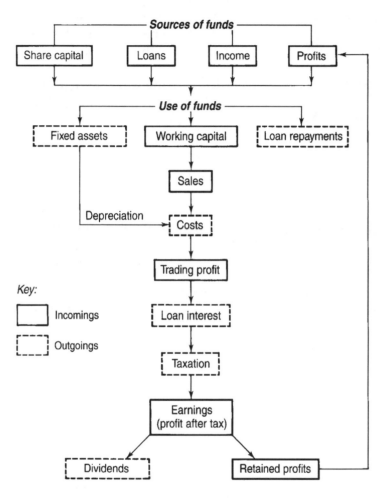

Figure 1.1 *The business system model*

share capital from investors, loans from banks and other institutions, and their own self-generated funds, their retained profits. In most instances, the money raised has to be accounted for and the loan eventually paid back. Businesses need funds to purchase assets such as factories, plant machinery, vehicles and equipment, and to pay the day-to-day bills such as rent, salaries and wages, the cost of raw materials and utilities.

Income

Leaving the Business System Model aside, let us now examine in more detail the income and outgoings of an average organisation. There are various types of income common to most organisations (although government-funded organisations may have only one source of revenue, the government, which in turn obtains the money from taxation).

Direct invoicing

Here the business sells goods and/or services to a third party (the customer) for cash, credit or a mixture of both. If credit, then the business will receive the money at a future date, as agreed with the customer in line with the terms and conditions of trading of the company; this is the most common form of 'money inwards' within the business system. Just a few minutes at a large supermarket checkout reminds us of the vast sums of money changing hands hourly.

Transfer pricing

In some large organisations, multinationals and conglomerates, there may well be several facilities, sites or factories, producing goods or partially finished goods which are then transferred to other parts of the business to continue the production process. In such cases, rather than go through the mechanisms of selling product from factory A to factory B, raising an invoice and then arranging payments, a process called transfer pricing is used.

Here the management enter into a pricing agreement to sell from factory A to factory B at a given price for a given period. All the accounts need record are the volumes of product transferred, expressed in financial terms, and recorded monthly, quarterly or whatever. The advantages of transfer pricing agreements are that the sellers are assured of their price and the users of the product are assured of their supply and can therefore budget and cost accordingly. Obviously if buyers expect the price of the goods to rise they may wish to enter into a longer-term fixed-price contract than if they expect the price of the product to fall. The oil producing industry, for example, uses transfer pricing within its own divisions, as raw materials called feedstocks resulting from oil production are transferred to chemical sites for the manufacture of plastics and other chemical products.

Sales of plant and other fixed assets

Fixed assets can become obsolete in one business yet saleable to another. For example, there is always a ready market for secondhand agricultural machinery. Fixed assets can also be sold for scrap. Sometimes if a company needs to raise money to reduce its debt, part of the rationalisation programme could well include sales of fixed assets. Although not part of the general trading or commerce of the business, selling assets can become a significant source of income for a company. In the UK, the Forte company recently sold off substantial assets in order to raise cash as part of its defence strategy against takeover by Granada. More spectacularly, we have seen some of the newly independent states of the former USSR selling off warships and tanks in order to invest in new peacetime industries.

Sundry revenue sales

Although not particularly significant for most business, some companies generate income by sundry sales, which can be part of a programme of destocking or a perk for employees. Many manufacturing and retail operations have a staff shop or offer discounts to staff and family, or hold annual sales at preferential prices. Sales of cut-price tickets to airline employees may not contribute greatly to the companies' revenue, but they no doubt play a part in motivating staff who enjoy cheap flights.

Extraordinary income

Where a company generates income from a special activity which it does not normally undertake, this is called extraordinary income and it is highlighted in the annual accounts, so that shareholders can appreciate that this is not normal income. One of the strangest items of extraordinary income we have come across was the pensioner who died and left an estate worth several thousands of pounds to 'that nice kind company who sent me a cheque every month', not realising that this was her pension entitlement left to her on the death of her husband. Companies that don't normally hedge their currency transactions may make a significant profit or loss on such trading and this might be shown in the accounts as an extraordinary item.

USE OF FUNDS

Outgoings – or use of funds – is, as might be expected, a much larger list than sources of funds. In this chapter, let's just touch on some major groupings. As we have said, companies raise money to start a business and to expand or continue the business. Some of this money will be appropriated to fixed assets, some will be in working capital (money to pay day-to-day bills), and some to repaying loans. The type of business determines its patterns of expenditure, as well as management decisions taken where there are options: for example, a taxi driver may purchase a cab (a fixed asset) or may elect to rent one instead (tying up less of his capital); the reasons for such choices will be examined later in this book.

Organisations mainly purchase assets to produce goods or services for the running of the business. However, perhaps it is worth pointing out here that some companies sometimes purchase interesting(!) assets such as racehorses and yachts for somewhat less obvious reasons!

Fixed assets

Fixed assets are the long-term assets purchased to allow the business to operate over time. Examples are factories, plant and machinery, office fixtures and equipment and computers. All these are outgoings to the business system and have to be financed, repaired, and eventually replaced. Fixed assets are discussed throughout the book and we shall be looking at how financial managers assist general managers in deciding what assets to purchase and their rate of depreciation (chapter 21).

Costs

Labour

Probably the most important resource of a company is one not shown in the balance sheet: the workforce: staff and management. In some organisations considerable sums of money are spent in training the workforce. The full-time labour force these days is regarded as a fixed cost, that is to say that employees are paid irrespective of the activity of the company. In some of the institutions in the City of London, employees are traded as a commodity. Salaries and wages, bonuses, pension contributions, N.I. and other overheads are a very significant outgoing to the business system, and people – like other assets – should be properly looked after and used in the most efficient manner. We'll be examining some of these costs and options – such as 'outsourcing' – in later chapters.

Materials

Most companies purchase materials of one form or another. Manufacturing companies purchase raw materials and/or partially finished goods and, using other factors of production such as labour, fixed assets, electricity, etc., will change them into finished goods for sale. Retail companies purchase finished goods for display and sale through their outlets. Hospitals purchase food, bandages, drugs, and so on, in order to provide a service to their patients.

Overheads

Fixed assets and materials are not enough to run a business. Organisations also incur expenses involved in changing materials into finished goods and distributing the finished goods to the marketplace. In the company's accounts, overheads are, for convenience, split into their two main categories: *Direct costs* are the costs directly concerned with the production of goods, or the creation of a service; *Indirect costs* are those costs that are not directly concerned with production, for example personnel and accountancy costs. These expenses are examined in more detail in the following chapters, particularly chapter 13.

Loan interest

Most companies, at some point, borrow money from banks, insurance companies, pension funds or some other lending institution. The lenders demand a rate of return for lending the money, called interest. The interest rate charged is calculated according to risk and the prevailing interest rates in the market. Interest is an outgoing to the business system, and has to be paid out from the income of the business. In later chapters, in particular chapter 17, we examine the pros and cons of various types of finance and the costs of such borrowings.

Other outgoings

Assuming that the company is making a profit, i.e. income from sales exceeds all costs including depreciation and interest on loans, then the last outgoings in the business system represent a dividing-up of these profits.

Firstly, the state gets its share of company profits through *taxation*, including corporation tax. Secondly, since businesses are accountable to their owners, the owners and/or shareholders will want a return on their investment, and companies with shareholders will accordingly distribute monies to shareholders by way of a *dividend*. Prudent companies will not distribute all of the available profit, but will keep a percentage as *retained profit* which is a source of funds for the business.

2

Understanding the Books

———◇———

THIS CHAPTER gives the non-financial manager an overview of how present financial computer systems have developed. It also sets out why we sometimes need to go to a very low level of detail for financial planning purposes. The danger of computer systems is that many people, financial and otherwise, rely on them without enough financial know-how. When this happens errors can be difficult to detect or correct, and the non-financial manager is often at a disadvantage in 'arguing' with the financial departments who – in our experience – are often covering their own ignorance of the real workings of the company with accountancy jargon. The gulf between the financial and the non-financial manager is often that they are talking about two seemingly different things: what is happening on the 'shop floor' and what that activity looks like in money terms – and neither knows how to talk the other's language. This overview provides a bridge over that gulf.

The non-financial manager also needs to be proactive, and make suggestions to financial departments for where output from the computer system can be made more meaningful in everyday use in individual departments. This chapter will help you gain a basic understanding of the foundation of bookkeeping on which those suggestions must be based.

THE ROLE of the accountant and the functions of accounting are often ill-defined, causing difficulties for many managers. The late 1980s and early 1990s have seen too much emphasis on accountants running companies.

Many of the criticisms of the restructured National Health Service have centred around its new focus on accountancy and finance-driven motives. Broadly speaking, accountants – when acting in the role of accountant – should not run companies. This is not to say that someone trained as an accountant cannot make an effective entrepreneur, managing director or manager at any level – indeed a background in finance is often a very good route towards those roles. But we should clearly separate the role from the person.

The role of the accountant must be as a *tool* of management rather than a *driver* of management. Companies which have put accountants in the driving seat are not as successful as those that have recognised the accountancy function correctly. When strategy planning is done only by accountants, creativity is lost.

Imagine the company as a human body; the analogy provides for some interesting viewpoints.

Management, and in particular the board of directors, can be likened to the brain. It receives data from all its external sensors: eyes, ears, nose, mouth and touch receptors. It collects the data, analyses it and makes decisions about the situation around it and how to respond. It also makes plans for the personal advance of the individual within the world as it perceives it and as it expects it to be.

The arms and hands can be likened to the workforce. It is the hands which are the primary manipulators of the world around us; they enact complex plans created by the human brain, according to our analogy creating the goods and services that management has dictated should be the core activity of the company. The fingers house important touch sensors which feed information back to the brain. To this extent the fingers can be likened to departments such as the sales force. The sales team are interfacing with customers and, if properly briefed, can bring information back to the management, enabling it to modify its plans according to the environment.

Money can be likened to blood. It circulates around the body, touching every part, taking energy throughout and bringing back exchange material in a never-ending circulation. There can be little doubt that money is the life blood of any company; a company dries up and dies without money as quickly as a body would without blood. Samples of blood, whether taken as part of a health check or in a specific investigation of a suspected illness, provide the doctor with a great deal of information. Analysis of the finances of a company provide no less information about the health and welfare of the company. But you cannot diagnose all illnesses only from the blood, and this provides our first caution against being overly dependent on accountants and finance.

Many companies have discovered that, for example, the customer complaints department could be likened to the body's pain sensors, providing the quickest and most unambiguous indication of something going wrong. Those companies which take note of messages from their customer complaints departments are the swiftest at correcting product defects and other problems.

However finance in a company is not just a life blood, it is also a measurement. Part of the rationale for this book is that to some degree even non-financial activities are reduced to financial measurement in order to fit them into the overall plans for the company which are usually, largely, expressed in financial ways.

The accountant, therefore, is not the brain of the company but the heart. Not the heart of a Valentine's Day card or the heart to which we ascribe emotion and expression, but rather the biological heart, the blood-pumping muscle. The human heart functions in ways which the brain dictates. All blood throughout the body passes through the heart, but the heart is not the reason for life, it is only one of many things that makes life possible. In the same way, the accounting department should be a tool of the board of directors, watching over all the cash flows but not becoming the driver of company activities.

Leaving this analogy behind and moving directly into the company structure, it is imperative that managers see accountants as a useful tool for the application of their decisions. In particular there must be a recognition, forced from management if necessary, that primarily the accountant produces data of use to the manager rather than the other way round. In fact the exchange of meaningful information must be both ways, and the end-user must decide the criteria.

No one would deny the importance of planning finances ahead and working towards that plan. However, in our experience the most successful companies have looked at their place in the business world, their products or services, and the degree of quality that they believe is appropriate, and their financial plans, (their expected profits and cashflows) are based on their product and quality-driven activities, and are not an end in themselves. Those companies which set out only with the primary goal of making profits are often short-lived or fall prey to buy-outs from those with longer-term ambitions. Hanson has made a corporate career out of identifying such companies!

The broad picture of this corporate circulatory system of financial information is shown in Figure 2.1 overleaf.

Source documents

These are basically external documents, or documents relating to external activities, which are the first input to the financial system. These would include: purchase invoices relating to goods and services the company has purchased; sales invoices relating to sales made to others; records of transactions not usually recorded by invoice, such as bank interest and charges; petty cash slips relating to small sundry purchases; and so on. These source documents come into the company through a variety of departments, in particular and most obviously the sales and purchasing departments, and they head towards the finance department for processing.

Books of prime entry

Books of prime entry record the source documents in a systematic way. Traditionally these would include:

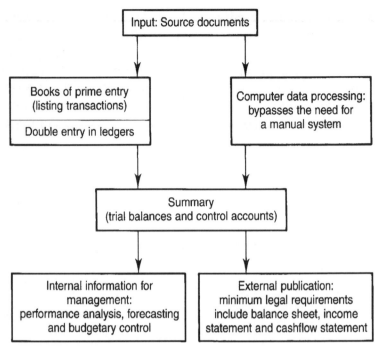

Figure 2.1   *Financial information: the corporate circulatory system*

▶ **A cash book:** reflecting transactions through the company's bank account by way of paying in, cheque payments, direct debit and standing order payments, bank drafts and so on. Specialist transactions recorded would include those transactions relating to import and export, often dealt with directly through the bank.

▶ **A petty cash book:** summarising the minor purchases by various people throughout the company. Ultimately sums listed in the petty cash book must match cheques shown in the cash book as having fed into the petty cash.

▶ **An expenses book:** some companies have a specific version of petty cash relating just to expenses of the sales force, directors and so on. Again, it is linked to the cash book which eventually pays the staff member for the expenses incurred.

▶ **The sales ledger / sales day book:** (a.k.a. receivables ledger and debtor's ledger – synonymous terms, used in some companies) these – two books, either one of which can be the book of prime entry with the other being a memo record relating to the sales the company makes. Generally speaking, the sales ledger is the book of prime entry recording each sale according to the customer. The sales day book records each sale made each day, week, month, etc. Obviously sales recorded in the two books should be equal over a period of time and the reconciliation between the two is one check that the documentation is being correctly processed. At any given time the balances on all the customer accounts in the sales ledger give us a figure of how much we are owed from customers, from sales or stage payments on long-term contracts.

▶ **The purchase ledger / purchase day book:** (Your company may call these the *bought ledger, payables ledger, creditors ledger* and *bought day book*.) Just as there are special books for sales, so there are equivalent books for purchases relating to the direct costs of manufacturing and selling the company's products. The two books are again reconciled, in the same way as the sales books.

▶ **A nominal ledger:** recording purchases relating to overheads rather than direct costs. Payments of electricity, telephone, rates, most salaries, and other overheads are recorded in the nominal ledger. This ledger has a 'page' for each overhead expense.

▶ **A journal:** Traditionally there is a book called the journal, which allows the information processors – the accountants and bookkeepers – to 'move' entries from one section of a book of prime entry to another, or from one book to another book. This might be for reallocation of costs or for correction of errors, and the movements are known as journal entries.

Double-entry bookkeeping

The basic rule which provides for error checking in accountancy is the principle of double entry. Under this principle, every transaction or activity is entered in two places in the books – once as a debit and once as a credit. There are two specific apparent anomalies that need to be explained here.

Firstly, when you, as an individual, think of your own bank account the bank tells you that you are in credit when you have money in the bank and that you have a debit balance when you are in overdraft. You need to remember that the terminology banks use reflects the point of view of *their* books rather than yours. In other words, when you have money deposited in the bank it is their liability, i.e. a *credit*, for them to repay to you. When you have an overdraft, a *debit*, you owe the bank money, the collection of which is to their advantage. For the moment, let's regard debits as assets, which are in the company's favour, and credits as liabilities which are *not* in the company's favour.

Secondly, profit appears on the balance sheet as a *credit*, i.e. equivalent to a liability. This would therefore seem to be 'bad' for the company whereas of course profit is actually good for the company. In accounting terms, the profit is owed back to the owners of the company, i.e. the shareholders, and can therefore be likened to a liability for accounting purposes.

Here are some examples of double-entry bookkeeping:

▶ If we sell one of the company's products for cash, then we record the sale as a *credit* in the sales ledger and the inflow of money as a *debit* to the cash book.

▶ If we make a purchase on credit, we record the purchase as a *debit* under that particular category of purchase in the purchase ledger; and record our liability to pay for it (as a creditor) in the purchase ledger. When it is paid for, the sum is *credited* in the cash book (i.e. paid from the bank) and *debited* in the purchase ledger. The debit and credit in the purchase ledger are equal and therefore balance each other off.

▶ If we take a loan from the bank to buy a building, we end up with a building and a liability to repay the bank. When we have acquired the asset of a building this is recorded as a *debit* in the 'buildings page' of the nominal ledger (i.e. good for the company) and the corresponding debt to the bank is recorded as a *credit* (i.e. a commitment the company must pay for).

There is no exception to this rule of 'every debit has a credit'.

Computer data processing

Virtually all large companies, and a great many smaller companies, now produce their accounts through computer systems, either tailormade or from a range of software packages available. Some of these maintain the terminology used above, others use clearer, every-day English to describe transactions. With the increasing use of simplified accountancy software, many people successfully process accountancy data without really understanding or seeing the double-entry system at work. However, the principles the computer uses are exactly the same as described above and exactly the same as will be described elsewhere in this book.

Probably the only modification that should be mentioned is that one characteristic of the computer is that it can make the entry in, say, the sales ledger in such a way that the sales ledger and the sales day book are actually only a method of organising and accessing data from the same entries rather than an actual update of two separate 'ledgers'. The same is true of the purchases system. But this is really only a background to the computer's way of accessing input data and not particularly essential for the end-user to appreciate.

Summary

Trial balances

Whether processed manually or by computer, the source data entered into the records are periodically brought together into a 'trial balance'. This takes all the summarised debit and credit entries and should produce an equal value of debit and credit on the basis that every transaction was matched by a counterpart under the double-entry system. Errors in the trial balance are therefore the first indication that some entry or other has been incorrectly dealt with and needs to be investigated.

In computerised systems there is usually some default arrangement for errors; the computer sends one side of a transaction here if it has not been fully instructed about it. This default is generally called a 'suspense account'. From here it must then be analysed again and reallocated by the accountants.

The end result is a list of the company's assets and a list of its liabilities, setting out the position at a particular moment in time. This set of balances eventually becomes the *balance sheet* – hence the expression – and will be examined in more detail in chapter 6.

Control accounts

Within the trial balance are certain accounts (mainly the sales ledger, purchase ledger and cash book) that will be 'controlled', i.e. reconciled and agreed back to source documents and to external confirmation. For example, the total list of balances which make up the sales ledger control account, i.e. the total amount of money owed to the company, can then be checked back to individual accounts for each customer and indeed confirmed directly with the customer to ensure that their books reflect the same position. Similarly with the purchases side.

A further reconciliation is to ensure that what we believe has been transacted through the bank has indeed happened. The cash book is reconciled to the bank statements to ensure all entries are correctly recorded. In order to ensure that the balances are correct, the reconciliation must take into account those entries entered in the cash book which have not yet been processed through the bank (i.e. the company may have issued a cheque but the payee has not yet paid it into the bank).

Internal information for management

Periodically, typically monthly in large companies, the data is collected together and circulated to management so they can use it as an indication of whether or not the performance of the company is as expected. This allows management to examine those areas which are not meeting their set objectives, and to discover whether or not improvements or modifications are needed. If we refer back to our diagram on page 14, it is this information used for performance analysis, forecasting and budgetary control. This internal information is highly confidential and contains a far greater degree of detail than the external, published company accounts, as obviously we do not want our competitors to have access to our best practices and the 'edge' which makes us competitive.

The internal information is generally known as 'quick and dirty', meaning that to some degree we can accept some inaccuracy in exchange for information which is very quickly available and on which we can make meaningful, quick decisions. Information that is highly accurate but presented too late means that management would be unable to react to information usefully.

This circulated internal data is used as a basis for forecasting, budgeting and planning and the new figures will then be the measure against which next month's output can be monitored, and new budgets, plans and forecasts created; and so the cycle continues.

External publication requirements

The law requires that a certain minimum level of information about the company is placed on the public record and made available to shareholders. While this information comes from the same source and the same accountancy records, a greater time is usually taken to make it more accurate than the management information. It is therefore essentially a historical record rather than an ongoing working tool. The published profit and loss and balance sheets are explained in chapters 5 and 6.

The external data, once published, is an end in itself and although it may be used by analysts to examine the company's public profile it has no further use internally.

3

The Accounting Concepts

---◇---

ONE OF OUR CLIENTS – a leading retail chain of jewellers – has the problem that the shop managers always want to value their stocks as highly as possible. As this valuation figure is a deduction from the costs of purchasing, the result is that the difference between costs and value is lower, and profit is higher. This means the manager gets an increased bonus. But the problem is that this leaves the stock potentially overvalued, and distorts a proper understanding of the company's performance. The company must reconcile the needs of the manager with the demands of law and common sense.

This is a typical area where the accountants rely on the non-financial managers for information. Unfortunately the information they get is often not meaningful to them because basic accounting needs are not understood by the non-financial manager. The rules have not been explained.

For their part, non-financial managers are able to offer a sensible judgment – within the accounting rules – of issues such as the length of useful life of certain assets (for which the non-financial manager may have expended part of his or her budget).

This chapter sets out the guidelines that should be followed by the finance departments in key areas, so that the non-financial manager can play a meaningful part in the flow of information.

IN CHAPTERS 5 and 6 you will see an example of a published profit and loss account and a balance sheet. In this chapter, we set out the basic rules which have developed to ensure their consistency.

In publishing accounts data, particularly for public file, a number of key concepts are used to ensure that like-for-like comparisons can be made between the accounts of a company over time and between all companies. Adherence to these concepts is not required for management's internal accounts (although many are based on common sense and should at least be considered when producing management figures).

If you are analysing the external accounts of another company, it's possible that any avoidance of the key concepts may reflect fraud or deliberate misrepresentation; but bear in mind that usually you will be trying to find the reality behind truthful figures rather than looking for fraudulent figures. Most companies seek to present their best impression and you will gain a truer picture if you can identify some of the figures which they would prefer not to highlight.

For example, a company may show debtors in its balance sheet at a given figure although it may know, or at least have a reasonably good idea, that some of those debts are not recoverable, i.e. that the company will not be paid. By questioning the degree of conservatism (prudence) that has been adopted we can see whether or not the figure presented is reasonable. We might also invoke the concept of consistency to see whether the same criteria has been applied this year to previous years. This might mean that if the company is seeking to increase its profits in this year it might not write off debts that it knows to be bad, which are for example over nine months old, although in previous years any debt over nine months old would have been written off and this gives us an indication that there may be a certain 'massaging' of the figures. Throughout this chapter, under the various 'concept' headings you will find other examples of typical considerations to bear in mind.

As a manager, you may be analysing the accounts of another company for a variety of reasons:

▶ Your company may be considering taking over another company and you may be asked to examine the financial reports relating to your particular field of expertise.

▶ You may be about to embark on a joint venture in, say, product development and you will want to be certain that they are likely to survive in the long term so that your investment is not wasted, or to ensure that you will not be asked to foot a higher percentage of the bill.

▶ You may simply be considering extending credit to the company and want some confirmation that the company is creditworthy.

'GOING CONCERN'

The concept of 'going concern' assumes that the company is a viable entity which will continue in operation into the future. Published accounts assume that all companies are a going concern unless specifically otherwise stated.

The going concern concept is an accounting and business judgement as to whether a company is likely to pay its bills and, indeed, survive in the short term. For example, you can spend £250,000 or more on building a theme pub, but only paying customers will make it a going concern.

If a company is *not* a going concern, it will need to be financially supported by an outside body – for example, a bank.

MATCHING

The concept of 'matching' ensures that payments made relate to the period covered. Adjustments are therefore made for prepayments and accruals (payments which you are expecting to make).

For example, and given a year end of 31 December, an insurance payment to cover the year 2000 might be made on

1 January 2000 and renewal of the same insurance for the year 2001 made on 31 December 2000. Without matching, the *profit and loss account* for the year ended 31 December 2000 would carry two insurance charges, whereas the profit and loss account for the year ended 31 December 2001 would carry none. The payment made on 31 December 2000 is therefore regarded as a payment in advance (or prepayment) and is carried forward through the *balance sheet* from the profit and loss account of 31 December 2000 into the profit and loss account for the year ended 31 December 2001. In the balance sheet at 31 December 2000 the payment will be shown as a payment in advance, one of the current assets.

Similarly, during the year ended 31 December 2000 the company may incur legal fees, perhaps as a result of a litigation. By 31 December 2000 the solicitors may not have raised an invoice as the litigation may be ongoing. Nonetheless, the company knows it has incurred a liability and will accrue a sum equal to the liability it believes it has incurred (by consulting with the solicitors if the cost cannot be accurately estimated). It charges that sum to the profit and loss account for the year ended 31 December 2000 and shows the sum as an accrual, i.e. similar to a creditor (see below), in the *current liabilities* of the balance sheet to 31 December 2000. When the payment is made during the year ended 31 December 2001, the payment will be matched against the brought-forward accrual rather than being charged into the profit and loss account for 31 December 2001.

Debtors and creditors are similar to the above, but relate to invoiced transactions. Creditors represent bills received by the balance sheet date, 31 December 2000 in our example, which relate to the year ended 31 December 2000 (so that the charges are shown in the profit and loss account for that year) but which are expected to be paid after the balance sheet date, i.e. in the year ended 31 December 2001. Similarly, debtors are sales a company has made to its customers during the year ended 31 December 2000 but for which the company has not yet received payment. It expects to receive payment during the year ended 31 December 2001. In both cases, when the payment is made (in the case of creditors) or received (in the case of debtors) during the year ended 31 December 2001, this will be set against the brought-forward creditor or debtor rather than recorded as a transaction of the year ended 31 December 2001.

By application of all these rules, the profit and loss accounts of each year should accurately reflect the sales, and the costs incurred in producing those sales, matched against each other and relating to the appropriate year.

CONSISTENCY

There must be consistency in treatment of items from one financial period to the next. For example, depreciation is the 'notional' write down of a fixed asset according to its expected normal life. If we assume that motor vehicles are believed to have a four-year life, then on a simple basis they would be written down by 25% per annum. If the motor vehicles cost £20,000, a charge of £5,000 would be set agaisnt the profits of the year for each of four years. However, if this policy were changed midway it would distort the declared profit. For example, if in the year ended 31 December 2000 a charge of £5,000 were set against the profits and in the following year to 31 December 2001 a change of policy depreciating the car by 50% would charge £10,000 against that year's profits, the profits of the two years would not be properly comparable.

There may be good reasons for changing the depreciation policy. For example, changes in technology might demand that a 25% write-down of computer equipment should be changed to a 50% write-down if the equipment is thought to be more rapidly becoming obsolete. In this case it would be appropriate to make the change. But in order that analysts, internally or externally, can make sense of the figures, the accounts must show the effect of the change clearly. To do this they must show what the depreciation charge and result-ant profit would have been had the previous policy been maintained, and must explain the reasons for the change of policy. The published accounts of limited companies contain the comparative figures for the previous year and a note to the accounts might show what the effect of the new depreci-ation policy would have been had it been applied to the previous year's figures.

This allows for flexibility in changing circumstances while at the same time providing for meaningful comparative infor-mation.

The valuation of stocks is another item where there might be reasons for changing the basis of valuation but again the consistency rules stipulate that it must be made clear in the notes to the accounts what the comparison between the two years would have been under the same policy. Stock could, for example, be valued (a) at the average of costs throughout the year, (b) at the value as at the balance sheet date or (c) at the value according to 'first in, first out', assuming that each item of stock sold is the oldest piece of stock purchased. Where the price of the stock is changing throughout the year, these various valuations would differ. There may be good reasons for changing the valuation, particularly of individual stock lines, but any material effects must be quantified.

MATERIALITY

This concept seeks to avoid wasting time on unnecessary and uneconomical precision. Almost all rules, concepts, controls, even calculations of figures, can be ignored if the effect is immaterial. Materiality may be defined as affecting a person's understanding of the figures. If, for example, a multinational company with hundreds of millions of pounds of turnover reported sales inaccurately by £10 then clearly there would be no effect on the understanding of that company's results or position by reading a figure plus or minus £10. There is no precisely quantifiable definition of materiality in terms of money, but there are some rules of thumb:

▶ Any figure inaccurate by 10% or more would certainly be regarded as being materially inaccurate and requiring correction.

▶ Any error of less than 1% in a figure would probably be regarded as immaterial.

▶ Between 1% and 10% the company, and probably its external auditors, would have to make a reasoned argument for whether an item was or was not regarded as material.

It must be borne in mind that the overall effect of examining the figures must be taken into account. An error of 1% in sales may be immaterial in an understanding of the turnover of the company but may still require correction in order to clarify its overall results. If the company produces a net profit of, say, only 3% then there would be a clear material effect on profit by a 1% error in sales.

CONSERVATISM (OR PRUDENCE)

The accounts must reflect the most conservative, i.e. prudent, of reasonable possibilities. For example, a profit must not be included in the profit and loss account until such time as it has been realised. A wholesaler might purchase a machine for resale, costing £3,000. The company knows that the market is such that it can sell that machine for £5,000 and therefore it has a potential profit of £2,000. However, it cannot take that profit into the profit and loss account until the sale is made.

On the other hand, the company might have bought a machine for £3,000 with the expectation of selling it for £5,000 but market forces, changes in technology, lack of foresight, or whatever, may mean that it now understands that it will not be able to sell the machine for more than

£2,000. This means that when it makes the sale it will incur a loss of £1,000. As soon as it identifies the potential for the loss then the item of stock is written down to £2,000, effectively taking the loss in the year in which it is recognised, whether or not the sale has yet been made.

The most obvious and commonly known use of the principle of conservatism is indeed in the valuation of stocks for sale; these are generally valued at 'the lower of cost or net realisable value'. This means that an item of stock will generally be shown at the cost at which it was purchased unless a lower sales value has been identified, in which case that figure will be substituted. The write-down of value in stock is charged to the profit and loss account in the year in which it is identified.

Between these two examples we can see that in either case the profit and loss account for a given year will be the most prudent, i.e. showing the minimum of profit. The balance sheet will also be the most prudent: in the case of stocks the valuation will reflect at most a value which is thought to be realisable.

COST

All transactions are based on *historical cost*. In the accounts, *sales* are shown at the invoice price and not uplifted or downgraded according to the price similar items would realise at the balance sheet date. Similarly, *costs* are shown at the actual amount paid or incurred in the period rather than what the cost might be at the balance sheet date. *Valuations* in the balance sheet are shown at the historical cost, i.e. fixed assets such as plant and equipment and cars are shown at the cost for which they were purchased regardless of their replacement cost or their true valuation if sold. *Debtors* are shown at the expected realisation figure, i.e. the invoice price less a provision for any potential bad debts (those invoices for which, for some reason, we do not expect to receive payment).

There is provision for the disclosure of current-cost

accounts in company accounts in addition to, not instead of, the historical-cost figures. Some companies feel that their true position is more accurately disclosed by using current-cost figures; this might mean that fixed assets and stock, for example, are shown at the price they would cost to replace rather than their original actual purchase price. However, in order that all accounts can be fairly compared, the historical figures must be shown also.

REALISATION

It is required that all short-term (current) assets designed to be converted into cash are capable of realising at least the value for which they are shown in the accounts.

Taking the case of debtors, the directors have a responsibility to ensure that the value of debtors shown in the balance sheet has a reasonable expectation of recovery; they should provide for bad debts where the value of items is not expected to be recovered. The bad debts provision in the accounts may be made up of specific bad debts known to be likely to be unpaid and a provision based on historical trends of, say, 2% of the total value of debtors, on the basis that this percentage is commonly not recovered year on year. The concept of realisation links the concepts of conservatism and cost to ensure that all potential losses are provided for.

4

Users of Accounts

---◇---

SEVERAL YEARS AGO one of the authors was asked, by a large client company for whom at that time we were consultants, to run a financial appreciation course for shop stewards and conveners. Wage negotiations were taking two to three weeks. It dawned upon the management that one of the major sticking points was that the union representatives had not had a chance to have the company's financial performance explained to them. Once this was done, the time taken over wage negotiations was halved (thereby justifying our fee)!

Accounts are used by many interest groups, all of whom have different, and sometimes conflicting, reasons for their understanding of the figures. As a manager, it may be your divisional or company accounts that these groups are examining, or you may be examining other companies' accounts. In order to gain a full appreciation of what is being shown, or concealed, you need to know why accounts present the information they do bearing in mind those who are reading them.

By the same token, after reading this chapter you will be better equipped to decide what information you want to present and what you would rather remained less visible.

IT IS important to stress at the outset that although some accounts are prepared fraudulently to conceal the truth about the figures, minimise tax unlawfully and so on, the majority of 'distortions' are either accidental or a genuine matter of particular presentation and usually represent a lawful choice between various presentation options. Your job is to read between the lines and behind the figures to gain a fuller appreciation of the truth. If you were being asked to verify a company's figures as part of a long-term joint development, for example, you might need to be sure that you concurred with their optimistic view of their own future; in short, you might or might not agree with some of the legitimate choices of presentation of the figures they offer you.

MANAGEMENT

Management's use of accounts has been mentioned in chapter 2. When decision-making, managers use internal accounts prepared to a lesser degree of accuracy, but much more quickly, and in far greater detail, than the external accounts made available to the public. These internal accounts contain many of the unpublished data discussed throughout this book.

Management do use the published accounts, however, in advertising and promoting the company. Accounts are often published in 'glossy brochure' form as part of presenting the company to the world at large; in addition to the figures they include statements of aspirations for the future by the chair or board of directors. In particular, the director's report is one opportunity for the company to spell out its long-term strategy and vision. The principal constraint is that the statements made must be consistent with, or at least not inconsistent with, the figures on which the director's report is commenting.

INLAND REVENUE AND CUSTOMS & EXCISE

These are the two principal government departments concerned with tax collection. They examine company accounts from the point of view of ensuring that the government is receiving its proper amount of taxation from the company.

The Inland Revenue deals with: corporation tax; PAYE (Pay As You Earn) relating to the directors, staff and work-force; the tax due on dividend payments; and less frequent taxes such as taxes on loans to directors, capital gains tax, and so on. The Inland Revenue is entitled to see more detailed accounts than are generally published and if they have reason to suspect concealment of figures leading to underpayment of tax they have the power to examine all the books and records of the business.

The Customs & Excise deal with import and export and are probably most visible for their administration of the collection of VAT (Value Added Tax). They are concerned to ensure that all VAT applicable on turnover is declared and that all claims to offset VAT on purchases against VAT on sales are valid. They therefore periodically examine detailed accounts and the books of prime entry (see chapter 2) to ensure that the company is complying with regulations.

CREDITORS

Here, 'creditors' mean the people to whom the company owes money. In the first instance, those proposing to offer the company goods on credit, i.e. on deferred payment, will examine the company's accounts to ensure that the company is likely to be able to meet its commitments. In particular, they will look at the working capital ratio and liquidity ratio (see chapter 8) to ensure that the company has the cash available to maintain its day-to-day commitments. Once they have accepted the company as a regular customer they should monitor the accounts to ensure that the company's working capital and liquidity do not worsen. If they discover that the company is becoming a higher risk, they may withdraw the credit they have previously offered, possibly to the extreme of demanding cash on delivery, or even cash with order. The published accounts are, for many companies, the only such source of information, with the obvious drawback that they are often 'too little too late'. For very large contractual commitments, written undertakings may be demanded and even some detailed management information provided by mutual agreement. Agencies (such as Dunn & Bradstreet) are sometimes employed to evaluate the creditworthiness of a company.

BANKS

Most companies borrow from banks to finance capital expenditure programmes, part of working capital, and so on. These borrowings may take the form of short-, medium- or long-term loans, debentures and/or overdrafts. The bank will examine the accounts of the company to ensure that their exposure through these forms of financing is not unduly risky. They will look to confirm that the ongoing trading position of the company is able to generate sufficient income to pay interest and charges and they will seek to ensure that the capital sums loaned are secured against either specific assets (such as a building) or the general assets of the company, and that the company has value in its assets to support its borrowings.

LOAN COMPANIES

Those lending the company money will want to consider the following questions:

▶ Why does the company need or want to borrow? For example, is it unable or unwilling to raise investment capital, i.e. share capital, perhaps because it has little faith in its ability either to increase the share value or to return dividends?

▶ How 'highly geared' is the company? This refers to the relationship between fixed-interest loans and equity. Does it already have fixed-interest loans which are draining its available day-to-day working capital because of loan interest repayments?

▶ Does the company have the *security* to back the size of the loan? The loan company may wish to take a charge over all the assets of the company, or over specific assets, particularly land and buildings if the loan is being used for their specific purchase.

▶ If the loan company is taking a floating charge over all the assets, it will want to know whether anyone else is 'first in the queue' with prior-lodged charges. If the company has given charges these will be registered on the public file at the Companies Registry.

▶ Has the company already sold off capital assets to raise cash and does it therefore have less security (fixed assets) than the last published balance sheet would indicate?

▶ Similarly, has the company converted its capital assets to leases, using sale and lease-back, or does it have an increased emphasis on *leasing* (which will mean it has fewer assets against which a charge can be effected)?

▶ Does the company have the ongoing day-to-day trading income sufficient to pay the loan interest? Loan companies do not want to recall loans, even though they take the security to enable them to do so if necessary.

▶ Will paying the loan interest restrict the future activities or growth of the company in a way that is, in the long term, detrimental and could reduce the value of the company, which would affect the secured assets?

▶ Some loans are issued in the form of debentures and this is generally contingent on the company reporting figures periodically to the loan company. In these cases, is the company reporting its monthly and/or quarterly figures regularly, and if not, why not? The assumption will be that if figures are not being presented something is being concealed.

▶ Is there information from outside the company that

suggests that the debenture reports are 'optimistic'? The bank, for example, sees the bank statements!

▶ For smaller companies, lenders will often require the personal guarantees of the directors or principals. Each guarantee will need to be supported by collateral, e.g. the director's house! Can these guarantees be obtained?

▶ Is the money being applied realistically by the company? Long-term loans should be applied to long-term assets and short-term loans to short-term working capital requirements. The company that takes a twenty-five-year mortgage for its car fleet is obviously going to have difficulties when it needs to replace the cars in three or four years' time!

Some of these considerations are also expanded in chapter 17, *Sources of Finance*.

SHAREHOLDERS

Shareholders are divided broadly into two groups: those who want capital growth and those who want income. Many, of course, are seeking a balance of the two.

Shareholders who are looking for long-term capital growth will be happy investing in companies that reinvest their profits into the long term. They will expect to see, in the company's development plans and in the current director's report, some indication of the long-term goals for which money that could be paid in dividends is being withheld. Obviously such investors will also look to the history of the company and be more content to invest in those that already have some track record of successful growth.

Investors who are seeking income will want to ensure that the company has a track record of issuing dividends. Some companies in fact squeeze their growth programme in order to pay dividends just to keep shareholders satisfied, and thereby to avoid a fall in the value of shares.

'Preference shares' are divided into those which are non-cumulative, i.e. if a dividend is not paid in the year then it is never to be paid, and cumulative, i.e. if a dividend is not paid that year then it rolls forward as a liability for future years. All dividends on preference shares must be paid before the ordinary shareholders can receive dividends. Where there is a mix of ordinary and preference shareholders, ordinary shareholders will be looking to see if a backlog of preference dividend is due; if so, there will be little rush to buy ordinary shares.

Shareholders will also want to ensure that there is not going to be an over-dilution in the value of their shareholdings by the influx of new investors, unless they feel that this will lead to an overall growth beneficial to all.

Many large shareholding blocks are advised by institutional investors, pension funds, portfolio managers, and so on, and they will be examining the company's historic record and future prospects very closely.

TRADE UNIONS AND EMPLOYEES

Those examining the accounts on behalf of employees, or the employees themselves, will be concerned with the following:

▶ To ensure that wage rises and/or restraints are fair and/or justified. In particular, existing employees and their representatives will be concerned to compare wage rates and wage rises with those of management using the staff salaries data. Large disparities can cause great controversy, as in the case of the recently privatised utilities.

▶ To ensure that future wages are secure for employees. The company which looks as if it is on a course for collapse is obviously of concern to its employees.

▶ To see that the company is not a prospect for takeover, or at least to be forewarned if it is; takeovers usually involve some redundancies and/or structural changes affecting staff.

If, for example, the total asset value of the company was, say, £1 million but all the share capital could be bought at the present market price of a total of £750,000, then the company might, taking this simplistic view, be ripe for a take-over or a predatory attack by an 'asset stripper' who would seek to buy the company cheaply, sell off its components and take a quick profit. The result in either case would be some or all redundancies for staff.

▶ To study trends and/or changes to ensure that redundancies are not round the corner because of planned growth, planned 'downsizing' and/or major technological investment. These things may be inevitable and the trade unions or the representatives of the employees will at least seek to forewarn people as early as possible and pressure the company for good redundancy packages, job relocation and/or constructive preparation for redundancy and retraining. A company may seek to hide its plans but the figures will tell the story in the end.

▶ Trade unions use the internal accounts information in wage negotiations where the company is insisting on some profitability criteria.

Although trade unions' interests are often perceived as being at odds with tough decisions relating to wages and/or staffing, this is not always the case. Just prior to the retirement, on 1 October 1996, of Jan Timmer – the chairman who successfully reversed the ailing fortunes of the multinational company Philips – the unions publicly praised his tough decisions as having saved the company from collapse, and thereby having ensured security for as many jobs as possible.

POTENTIAL TAKEOVER BIDDERS

A bidder, often a large public company, which is seeking to buy out another company, will be particularly looking for companies whose assets are undervalued because it can buy cheaply and possibly then dispose of the assets (this is known as asset stripping). The potential bidder will be interested in:

▶ the true value of assets, compared with the balance sheet values;

▶ the financial and dividend policy, and the resultant share-holders perceptions;

▶ the value of the shares as quoted on the Stock Exchange, compared with the underlying net asset value;

▶ assets which can be turned into cash quickly; in particular, trade investments, and prime-site land and buildings;

▶ companies which under-utilise resources and have built up large cash balances for other immediate liquidity positions.

FINANCIAL ANALYSTS

Many sharp and experienced financial analysts examine company accounts on behalf of investors and other interested parties. They use certain key performance ratios to determine management effectiveness, public perception, and so on. You will find detailed examples of these accounting ratios in chapter 8. For the moment, here are three of the basic calculations.

Earnings per share (EPS)

This is calculated as follows:

$$\frac{\text{Profit after tax (in pence)}}{\text{Number of shares issued}}$$

Example:

$$\frac{90,000 \text{ pence}}{1,000} = 90\text{p per share (or 90\%)}$$

This means that for every £1 share there is a potential 90p return in dividend if all the profit after tax is to be distributed to shareholders.

This ratio is used by external analysts to determine whether they wish to invest in a company, or wish to advise their clients to invest, based on the likelihood of dividend return. Some financial analysts examine companies to determine those shares which are likely to offer their clients long-term growth and therefore capital gains, and those which are likely to return short-term dividend income.

Dividend ratio

This shows the proportion of income actually paid in dividends, as opposed to what was available. It is calculated as follows:

$$\frac{\text{Dividends per share}}{\text{Earnings per share}}$$

To continue the above example, and with a proposed dividend being £500 on £1,000 of ordinary shares of £1, this ratio would be:

$$\frac{50 \text{ pence}}{90 \text{ pence}} = 0.56 \text{ to } 1$$

Movements in this trend show management's decision to make available to shareholders a certain proportion of what is available to them, the remainder presumably being reinvested into the longer term. As with the earnings-per-share ratio, this will give some indication to investors of the likelihood of capital growth as opposed to short-term income.

Price/earnings ratio (P/E ratio)

This is calculated as follows:

$$\frac{\text{Market price of share}}{\text{Earnings per share}}$$

Continuing our example, and with a Stock Market share price of £2, this would be:

$$\frac{200p}{90p} = 2.2 \text{ to } 1$$

Each share is valued at 2.2 times its EPS figure. This means that by investing £200 in 100 shares shareholders could expect to receive £90 in the first year, £90 in the next year, and so on, with the investment still intact.

These figures (used again in the example in chapter 8) have been deliberately exaggerated to show the calculation. (In reality the Stock Exchange would be swamped immediately on opening should a company ever come onto the market in this state – there would be buyers but no sellers!)

Obviously financial analysts look at the price earnings ratio along with these other last ratios in order to determine the true value of investment in your company.

Remember that the importance of the ratios is not the individual figure produced at any one time but the analysis over time, the comparison against expectation. They help in examining how accurately a company is performing to its plans and inter-firm comparison with similar businesses in the industry.

Bear in mind that only directors get the detailed analysis of how the profit or loss figure is calculated, as this is sensitive information, whereas the shareholders are restricted to the published figures as filed at Companies House.

5

The Profit and Loss Account

ONE OF the most frequently seen financial statements is the profit and loss account, or income and expenditure statement. This sets out the income and expenditure, and resulting profits, over a period – usually a month or quarter in management figures. it is a summary of information from all departments in a company, and a basic source of information for cost control and financial planning. A version of the profit and loss account, usually giving figures for a whole year, is also available on public record at Companies House and is available for anyone to examine. This provides for an easy access to summarised information about the company. Interim, usually half-yearly, results are published by many large companies as information to shareholders.

THE PROFIT AND LOSS account measures the sales and other trading income, the expenses incurred to make that income, and the resultant net profit. Broadly speaking, it does not indicate the long-term thinking of management (though individual heads of expenditures may well give an indication in the notes against certain entries).

Figure 5.1 shows a typical profit and loss account as would be seen in the published accounts of a major company. (In this example, the company is the holding company of a group and therefore the figures shown are the consolidated, i.e. totalled, results for the group, together with the previous year's comparatives as required by law.) Deductions and losses are shown in brackets.

for the year ended 31 March	1999 £m	1998 £m
Turnover	5200	4700
Operating costs before exceptional items	(3900)	(3600)
Exceptional items: charged against operating costs	(60)	–
	(3960)	(3600)
Total operating costs	1240	1100
Operating profit		
Other exceptional items:		
Profits less losses on sale and termination of operations	(20)	–
Losses on disposal of fixed assets	(40)	–
Provision for goodwill charge on impending sale of a business	(180)	–
Profit on ordinary activities before associated undertakings and minorities	1000	1100
Associated undertakings	(40)	(15)
Net interest and other similar income	(12)	10
Profit on ordinary activities before taxation	948	1095
Taxation	(250)	(230)
Profit on ordinary activities after taxation	698	865
Dividends – interim	(60)	(55)
– final (proposed)	(140)	(120)
Profit for the year retained	**498**	**690**

The group has made no acquisitions nor discontinued any operations within the meaning of Financial Reporting Standard 3 during either 1999 or 1998. Therefore turnover and operating profit derive entirely from continuing operations.

Figure 5.1 *Consolidated profit and loss account (HI-TECH PLC)*

EXPLANATION OF TERMS

(The more common terms are explained in *Parlez-vous Accountancy?* at the end of the book.)

Turnover

This word derives from 'stock turnover', i.e. the amount of times that the company uses and replaces its stock. It is a word for sales and/or income. It usually refers to the income derived by trading or manufacturing companies rather than by service industries.

Operating costs before exceptional items

The normal running costs of the company. This will be further broken down in the notes to the accounts into several categories including direct costs, administration costs, overhead costs, and so on.

Exceptional items

These are unusually large transactions, purchases or sales, where the company normally engages in that sort of transaction but where the size of the transaction is unusual. (For example, a bakery which traditionally sells a million rolls a year but which gets a one-off order for 10 million rolls for one particular transaction would regard this as an exceptional item as it is not likely to be repeated.)

Occasionally there is an entry for *extraordinary items*, which refers to activities that the company does not normally engage in. (For example, a bakery that for some reason buys and sells a ship and does not intend to move into the ship retailing business would regard the profits on the sale of a ship as an extraordinary item.)

Operating profit

This is turnover less total operating costs (including any exceptional operating costs).

Profit on ordinary activities before associated undertakings and minorities

This refers to the profit of the main company or group of companies.

Associated undertakings

This refers to the profits or losses of companies partly owned by the main company or group for which some of the profits or losses are attributable to the main company or group.

Taxation

Amounts due to the Inland Revenue for corporation tax.

Dividends

Amounts paid to shareholders as a return on their investment in the company. *Interim dividends* are payments made during the year and the *final dividend* is made at the year end following establishment of the results for the year.

6

The Balance Sheet

Another of the most frequently seen financial statements is the balance sheet. The balance sheet represents a 'snapshot' of a company's finances at one moment of time. By the following day the figures will have changed: debtors will have paid money, the bank balances will have changed, money will have been spent out of petty cash, stocks will have been sold, etc. At the end of each period of trading, a balance sheet shows the accumulated result of that period on the long-term assets and working capital. The balance sheets for two consecutive years are therefore 'bridged' by the profit and loss account. Any period of trading (one week, one month, one quarter, one year, or whatever) starts with an opening balance sheet and ends with a closing balance sheet. Management accounts may show the balance sheets (or key extracts) monthly; published accounts show an annual balance sheet at the company's year end.

INDIVIDUAL components of the balance sheet are studied in various sections throughout this book, but here we give a general introduction. Figure 6.1 shows a typical balance sheet as would be seen in the published accounts of a major company. In this example, the company is the holding company of a group and therefore there is an individual set of figures and a group set, each with the previous year's comparatives as required by law.

at 31 March	Group 1999 £m	Group 1998 £m	Company 1999 £m	Company 1998 £m
Fixed assets				
Tangible assets	5000	4500	150	125
Intangible assets	400	350	100	75
Investments	300	250	1100	1025
	5700	5100	1350	1225
Current assets				
Stocks and Work in progress	150	90	1	–
Debtors – due within one year	850	800	250	200
– due after more than one year	200	200	50	40
Current asset investments	40	–	30	–
Short-term deposits	900	1000	450	650
Cash at bank and in hand	100	90	5	2
	2240	2180	786	892
Current liabilities				
Creditors: amounts falling due within one year				
Loans and obligations under finance leases	(320)	(360)	(20)	(4)
Other creditors	(1450)	(1300)	(300)	(250)
	(1770)	(1660)	(320)	(254)
Net current assets	470	520	466	638
Total assets less current liabilities	6170	5620	1816	1863
Creditors: amounts falling due after more than one year				
Other loans and obligations under finance leases	(1200)	(1100)	(250)	(270)
Other creditors	(190)	(190)	(162)	(170)
Provisions for liabilities and charges				
Deferred taxation	(140)	(130)	(20)	(19)
Other provisions	(90)	(30)	(15)	(20)
	(1620)	(1450)	(447)	(479)
Net assets	4550	4170	1369	1384
Equity capital and reserves				
Called up share capital	550	545	550	545
Share premium account	380	360	380	360
Associated undertakings	1120	965	–	–
Profit and loss account	2500	2300	439	479
Equity shareholders' funds	4550	4170	1369	1384

Figure 6.1   *Balance sheet of a group holding company (RARE GAS PLC)*

EXPLANATION OF TERMS

(See also *Parlez-vous Accountancy?* for the more common terms.)

Fixed assets

The long-term assets of the company which it needs in order to operate (buildings, equipment, etc.), as opposed to its stocks and for current assets which may be bought and sold on a day-to-day basis.

Tangible assets

Physical assets such as cars, plant and machinery, and equipment. Classed as fixed assets.

Intangible assets

Goodwill, patents and copyrights – not physical assets but nonetheless long-term assets from which the company can generate income. For example, if a company owns a copyright it can sell a licence to another company to print the copyright material, and this generates income in royalties. Classed as fixed assets.

Investments

The company's long-term stake in other companies.

Current assets

Those assets which are expected to be continually turned over and may change many times during the course of the year.

Stocks

Physical goods held for resale or products used in the manufacture of goods for sale.

Work in progress

Companies which manufacture their products for sale will have a certain amount of semi-manufactured work at any given time; this is called 'work in progress'. Work in progress can take many forms: in the case of a profession it may be incomplete assignments for which no invoices have yet been raised on the work done to date.

Debtors

Amounts owed to the company by people to whom credit has been given for sales. The balance sheet distinguishes between those debtors due within one year and those due after a period of more than one year.

Current asset investments

Short-term investments held speculatively, which may be bought and sold very quickly.

Short-term deposits

Money invested in bank accounts, overnight deposits, and so on, to earn maximum interest but subject to continual monitoring and change.

Cash at bank and in hand

Basically the company's bank and petty cash balances.

Current liabilities

The short-term, day-to-day debts of the company which it expects to pay within one year.

Creditors

Those people to whom the company owes money for purchases where a credit period has been agreed.

Loans and obligations under finance leases

Basically, versions of commitments under hire purchase. Under 'current liabilities', these are the loans due within one year. Any remaining amounts are shown lower down the sheet, as 'Other loans and obligations ...'

Net current assets

This is the company's 'working capital', the money available to continue the day-to-day business.

Deferred taxation

A tax liability that is not expected to be paid, but might be paid if certain events were to come to pass. For example, the difference between the value of assets shown in the accounts and the value that is acceptable to the tax authorities. (Taxation regulations are beyond the scope of this book.)

Issued share capital

A company has an authorised share capital which is the amount of share capital it can issue but it may issue less; the degree to which it actually has issued shares to shareholders is known as its issued share capital.

Share premium account

When a shareholder buys a share there may be a premium to pay, i.e. an extra price for the benefit of buying that share. A £1 share may cost £3, therefore the £2 is the premium being paid. The extra money over and above the nominal figure (£1), is shown in the share premium account.

Profit and loss account

The accumulated profits, less losses, to date since the company's inception. This figure is transferred to the balance sheet.

BEYOND THE BALANCE SHEET

There is another way to consider the 'bridge' between two balance sheets. This ignores the profit and loss account and the profits made in that period, and considers the uses to which the profit has been applied. Figure 6.2 shows an example of a company's opening and closing balance sheets. The company has made a profit of £65,000. But we must ask ourselves if the profit made has been spent wisely for its short- medium- and long-term future. What the company has effectively done is:

▶ invested £70,000 into long-term assets;

▶ invested £25,000 into stock;

▶ allowed debtors a 'loan' of £20,000;

▶ paid for the above by using profits, running higher creditors, and exhausting cash supplies so that it needs an overdraft.

One analysis of this bridge, or movement, between balance sheets may be that the company has adopted a programme of long-term investment which may be useless if it cannot

	Opening balance sheet £	Closing balance sheet £	Movement £
Fixed assets			
Freehold buildings	40,000	80,000	40,000
Plant / Equipment	20,000	50,000	30,000
Current assets / liabilities			
Stock	15,000	40,000	25,000
Debtors	–	20,000	20,000
Cash	25,000	(10,000)	(35,000)
Creditors	(25,000)	(40,000)	(15,000)
	£75,000	£140,000	£65,000
Represented by:			
Share capital	75,000	75,000	–
Retained profit	–	65,000	65,000
	£75,000	£140,000	£65,000

Figure 6.2 *The movement of assets and liabilities during a trading period*

survive in the short term. It has not recognised that a proportion of profit must be reinvested into working capital. It now may not be able to buy the goods and services and pay the wages to continue its day-to-day business.

There are alternative possibilities. The company may have just begun an expansion programme based on sound analysis and backed by its bankers. The investment into long-term assets may be strategically sound, and the need for short-term working capital might be met out of agreed bank borrowings.

This kind of analysis therefore does not provide answers; but it provides you with some pertinent questions.

7

Cashflow

———◇———

KEVIN HAD JUST *been given a departmental budget of £250,000 per annum. He could see immediately that the department needed to spend some money on up-to-date equipment. The budget had been approved, and now the decision was his. So he kept back the £50,000 he knew he needed for day-to-day costs and committed £200,000 to one cheque for new computer equipment. But the requisition for the cheque was refused by the Finance Director on the grounds that the money was not yet available. Kevin was very embarrassed! He had just learnt that what you spend is only part of the equation; you need to plan for when you spend it.*

IN THE medium-to-long term, a business must be profitable in order to survive. If it does not produce an excess of income over expenditure it may survive for a time by borrowing money or taking injections of cash from speculating investors, but in the end the purpose of the business is to generate profits which enable it to stand alone and indeed to invest back into the company for future growth.

In the short term, even a profitable business can be brought down by adverse cashflow. Probably the most important recognition of the last five to ten years is that cashflow is, and should be, one of the principal, if not *the* principal, concern of effective management strategy. (It is significant that the key performance indicator, that most successfully predicts bankruptcy, is the liquidity ratio or 'acid test' which gives an indication of a company's ability to pay its way day-to-day – see chapter 8.)

As a non-financial manager you may have to offer cash-flow forecasts for inclusion into the master budgets. You must then 'call off' money according to that agreed plan in order not to cause the company as a whole financial difficulties, and to allow all departments access to what funds are available at any given moment in time.

The difference between profit and cashflow can be very simply explained in the following example, which also indicates how even a profitable company can bankrupt itself. A company buys an item for £500 on 1 August. It sells that same item for £800 two weeks later on 15 August. During the month of August the company has therefore made a profit of £300. The profit and loss account is:

	£
Sales price	800
Less costs	(500)
Profit	300

However, now let us examine those transactions more carefully. When we purchased the item on 1 August we agreed to pay for it on 1 September, one month later. When we sold the item on 15 August we made an agreement with our customers that they could pay for the item on 15 October, two months later. The result, in the case of this single transaction, is that on 1 September, when we have to pay for the purchase, we have not yet been paid for the sale; we have no sums available, and go bankrupt.

Note also that our profit and loss account showing a profit of £300 in the month of August is still correct; even the most sophisticated profit and loss account does not give an indication of cashflows. In reality, the complexity of ongoing purchasing and selling often masks poor cashflow for some months and occasionally even for years. However, every house of cards will fall in the end; only if a more positive cashflow is maintained will the structure hold.

The cashflow is a form of budget; it predicts inflows and outflows of cash for a period ahead. A typical proforma layout for a cashflow is shown in Figure 7.1. This is the most general of proformas, covering most of the basic inflows and outflows of the business. It would suffice, probably without amendment, for most small businesses and would be equally suitable as the overview cashflow document for a large business. But in large businesses there may also be departmental or divisional versions, all of which would feed into the main cashflow budget. Each department or division would, of course, have its own specific headings of income and expenditure.

You can use the cashflow proforma in Figure 7.1 to carry out an exercise. At the end of this exercise, you should be able to:

▶ complete a full year's cashflow chart;

▶ calculate the closing (December) bank balance;

▶ discover the points of highest and lowest liquidity for this year.

Exercise: part one

You will note that there are two columns for each month, headed 'Forecast' and 'Actual'. For the moment let us assume that you are considering figures somewhere towards the end of this year and are about to summarise your anticipated cashflow for next year. You will therefore be completing the Forecast column.

The following is the forecast data that you have obtained from within your company:

1. Credit sales

(this year:)
Nov   £2,500
Dec   £2,600
(next year:)
Jan   £2,700   Apr   £3,300
Feb   £1,800   May   £2,500
Mar   £3,900   Jun   £3,700

Jul	£1,800	Oct	£1,500
Aug	£1,200	Nov	£2,700
Sep	£1,300	Dec	£2,800

Payment is received two months after these invoice dates.

2. Cash sales

(next year:)

Jan	£500	Jul	£300
Feb	£200	Aug	£200
Mar	£300	Sep	£300
Apr	£400	Oct	£600
May	£600	Nov	£200
Jun	£200	Dec	£400

3. Opening bank balance is £1,000

4. Interest earned quarterly

(next year:)

Mar	£30
Jun	£40
Sep	£20
Dec	£80

5. Sundry income

(next year:)

Apr	£20 cash
Jul	£60 – to be received the following month

6. VAT due or recoverable

(next year:)

quarter ended	Jan	£200 due
quarter ended	Apr	£300 due
quarter ended	Jul	£200 due
quarter ended	Oct	£300 recoverable

The VAT office settles, and expects settlement, by the end of the following month.

Year:	January Forecast	January Actual	February Forecast	February Actual	March Foreecast	March Actual	April Forecast	April Actual	May Forecast	May Actual	June Forecast	June Actual
Opening bank balance b/fwd												
Income												
from Sales (cash)												
from Sales (debtors)												
from Interest earned												
from VAT recoverable												
from Other sources (sundry)												
Income subtotal												
Expenditure												
for Purchases (cash)												
for Purchases (on credit)												
Salaries and wages (Net)												
NI and PAYE												
Rent/Rates												
Light/Heat/Telephone												
Interest charges												
HP payments												
VAT payments												
Advertising, promotions												
Capital expenditure												
Other (specify)												
—												
—												
Dividend payments												
Expenditure subtotal												
Closing bank balance c/fwd												

Year: _____	July Forecast	July Actual	August Forecast	August Actual	September Forecast	September Actual	October Forecast	October Actual	November Forecast	November Actual	December Forecast	December Actual
Opening bank balance b/fwd												
Income												
from Sales (cash)												
from Sales (debtors)												
from Interest earned												
from VAT recoverable												
from Other sources (sundry)												
Income subtotal												
Expenditure												
for Purchases (cash)												
for Purchases (on credit)												
Salaries and wages (Net)												
NI and PAYE												
Rent/Rates												
Light/Heat/Telephone												
Interest charges												
HP payments												
VAT payments												
Advertising, promotions												
Capital expenditure												
Other (specify)												
–												
–												
Dividend payments												
Expenditure subtotal												
Closing bank balance c/fwd												

Figure 7.1 Cashflow proforma

7. Purchases for cash

(next year:)

Jan	£100	Jul	£200
Feb	£200	Aug	£100
Mar	£50	Sep	£300
Apr	£200	Oct	£400
May	£50	Nov	£500
Jun	£600	Dec	£100

8. Purchases on credit

(this year:)

Oct	£700	May	£600
Nov	£600	Jun	£800
Dec	£500	Jul	£900
(next year:)		Aug	£1,000
Jan	£900	Sep	£900
Feb	£800	Oct	£800
Mar	£700	Nov	£700
Apr	£500	Dec	£600

Each month's liabilities are settled in the third month after the end of the month in which they arise.

9. Net wages due per month: £200

The National Insurance and PAYE is £70 per month, due in the month following the wages payments.

10. Rent and rates

(next year:)

Mar	£1,500
Jun	£1,000
Sep	£1,500
Dec	£1,000

11. *Light, heating and telephone*

Invoices received:
(this year:)
Dec   £300
(next year:)
Mar   £400
Jun   £150
Sep   £200

These bills are paid in the month following the invoice month.

12. *Interest payable: £100 per quarter, starting March next year*

13. *Hire purchase (HP) payments: £50 per month*

14. *Advertising and promotions*

(next year:)
Feb   £50
Mar   £60
Apr   £70
May   £70

15. *Capital expenditure*

The company will contract in May next year for capital expenditure of £3,000. The item will be delivered in June next year, invoiced in July, and paid in August.

16. *Dividends*

(planned for next year:)
Mar   £3,000
Jun   £4,000
Sep   £3,000
Dec   £3,000

First, insert into the proforma cashflow the data you have been given. Then check it against the completed chart in Figure 7.2.

Consider some points arising from the translation of the data into the proforma:

Net wages, NI and PAYE

Including these figures is something of a red herring in this case. Where figures are constant the resulting cashflow forecast will reflect that.

Hire purchase

The hire purchase entry is designed to demonstrate one difference between cashflow forecast and profit and loss forecast. The £50 per month paid to a hire purchase company will contain elements both of capital repayment and of interest repayment. Only the interest repayment would be reflected in the profit and loss account as a charge for the period, whereas the capital repayment would reduce the hire purchase liability that would be reflected on the opening balance sheet. However, for the purposes of cashflow this is irrelevant: it is the £500 which will come out of the bank each month and, regardless of its make-up, this is the amount that must be shown in the cashflow forecast.

Capital expenditure

This information, while illustrating the various times which might be regarded as 'contractual' in terms of the expenditure, also shows that there is only one relevant date for a cashflow forecast and that is the date of payment, in this case August.

Dividends

As well as, or instead of, dividends, other payments to be

considered might typically be interdepartmental transfer payments or, in the case of an unincorporated small business, the money the proprietor draws out as his or her own salary.

From the completed cashflow chart, you can see that the bank balance at the end of May is £4,800 and the closing balance at the end of December is £4,460 overdrawn. These are the points of highest and lowest liquidity. We can immediately see one of the benefits of the cashflow forecast. By predicting times when there is surplus cash to hand we can be prepared to transfer cash from our current account to accounts earning higher interest, maximising our financial use of this resource. By predicting the times when the company will be in overdraft, and by calculating the maximum overdraft required, we can present our requirements to the bank ahead of time. Companies which demonstrate to the bank that they are able to predict their requirements are more likely to be regarded as a worthwhile risk than those which produce figures unexpectedly, and go to the bank in crisis rather than in anticipation.

Exercise: part two

Now let us suppose that a few months have passed and you have 'actual' data for the first three months of the year. This is the data you can now insert into the cashflow chart:

1. *Credit sales*

Nov	£2,500
Dec	£2,800
Jan	£3,800

As expected, payment has been received two months after these invoice dates.

2. *Cash sales*

Jan	£650
Feb	£170
Mar	£920

Year: _____	January Forecast	January Actual	February Forecast	February Actual	March Forecast	March Actual	April Forecast	April Actual	May Forecast	May Actual	June Forecast	June Actual
Opening bank balance b/fwd	1000		2580		4010		1510		1840		4800	
Income												
from Sales (cash)	500		200		300		400		600		200	
from Sales (debtors)	2500		2600		2700		1800		3900		3300	
from Interest earned					30						40	
from VAT recoverable							20					
from Other sources (sundry)												
Income subtotal	3000		2800		3030		2220		4500		3540	
Expenditure												
for Purchases (cash)	100		200		50		200		50		600	
for Purchases (on credit)	700		600		500		900		800		700	
Salaries and wages (Net)	200		200		200		200		200		200	
NI and PAYE	70		70		70		70		70		70	
Rent/Rates	300				1500		400				1000	
Light/Heat/Telephone					100						100	
Interest charges	50		50		50		50		50		50	
HP payments			200						300			
VAT payments			50		60		70		70			
Advertising, promotions												
Capital expenditure												
Other (specify)												
—												
—												
Dividend payments					3000						4000	
Expenditure subtotal	1420		1370		5530		1890		1540		6720	
Closing bank balance c/fwd	2580		4010		1510		1840		4800		1620	

Year:	July Forecast	July Actual	August Forecast	August Actual	September Forecast	September Actual	October Forecast	October Actual	November Forecast	November Actual	December Forecast	December Actual
Opening bank balance b/fwd	1620		3250		2990		(910)		(930)		(1020)	
Income												
from Sales (cash)	300		200		300		600		200		400	
from Sales (debtors)	2500		3700		1800		1200		1300		1500	
from Interest earned					20							
from VAT recoverable									300			
from Other sources (sundry)			60								80	
Income subtotal	2800		3960		2120		1800		1800		1980	
Expenditure												
for Purchases (cash)	200		100		300		400		500		100	
for Purchases (on credit)	500		600		800		900		1000		900	
Salaries and wages (Net)	200		200		200		200		200		200	
NI and PAYE	70		70		70		70		70		70	
Rent/Rates					1500						1000	
Light/Heat/Telephone	150											
Interest charges					100		200				100	
HP payments	50		50		50		50		50		50	
VAT payments			200									
Advertising, promotions									70			
Capital expenditure			3000									
Other (specify)												
–												
–												
Dividend payments					3000						3000	
Expenditure subtotal	1170		4220		6020		1820		1890		5420	
Closing bank balance c/fwd	3250		2990		(910)		(930)		(1020)		(4460)	

Figure 7.2 Cashflow exercise: answer, part one

3. *Opening bank balance is £1,000*

4. *Interest earned in March: £35*

5. *Sundry income nil in quarter*

6. *VAT for quarter ended January: £210 due*

7. *Purchases for cash*

Jan   £120
Feb   £240
Mar   £460

8. *Purchases on credit*

Oct   £700
Nov   £650
Dec   £700

9. *Net wages due per month*

Jan   £200
Feb   £200
Mar   £250

National Insurance and PAYE are £70 per month, as forecast.

10. *Rent and rates*

Mar   £1,500

11. *Light, heating and telephone*

Invoice received December: £320 (paid in January)

12. *Interest payable: £80 in March*

13. *HP payments: £50 per month*

14. *Advertising and promotions*

Feb   £250
Mar   £300

15. *No capital expenditure in quarter*

16. *Dividend, as planned paid in March: £3,000*

This data, inserted alongside the previously forecast data, produces the chart shown in Figure 7.3. You can now compare the first three months' actual cashflows with your expected cashflows. You will not be so concerned where your predictions were fairly accurate; for example, predicted cash sales for February were within a reasonable range of the actual results. In addition, there are certain predictions which you know will be accurate from the outset, for example rent and rates are usually predetermined months and, in the case of rent, often years ahead. However, you should look at those areas where there is considerable diversity from your forecast figures. This is known as 'exception reporting', i.e. devoting your attention to those areas where there is the maximum difference from what you expected. Let's look at some of these.

Cash sales

Cash sales in March were £920 whereas you had expected them to be only £300. There may be several factors involved and your understanding of these will enable you to better anticipate the year ahead. A few of the possible explanations are:

Year:	January Forecast	January Actual	February Forecast	February Actual	March Forecast	March Actual	April Forecast	April Actual	May Forecast	May Actual	June Forecast	June Actual
Opening bank balance b/fwd	1000	1000	2580	2690	4010	1990	1510		1840		4800	
Income												
from Sales (cash)	500	650	200	170	300	920	400		600		200	
from Sales (debtors)	2500	2500	2600	2800	2700	3800	1800		3900		3300	
from Interest earned					30	35					40	
from VAT recoverable							20					
from Other sources (sundry)												
Income subtotal	3000	3150	2800	2970	3030	4755	2220		4500		3540	
Expenditure												
for Purchases (cash)	100	120	200	240	50	460	200		50		600	
for Purchases (on credit)	700	700	600	650	500	700	900		800		700	
Salaries and wages (Net)	200	200	200	200	200	250	200		200		200	
NI and PAYE	70	70	70	70	70	70	70		70		70	
Rent/Rates					1500	1500					1000	
Light/Heat/telephone	300	320					400					
Interest charges					100	80					100	
HP payments	50	50	50	50	50	50	50		50		50	
VAT payments			200	210	60	300	70		300			
Advertising, promotions			50	250					70			
Capital expenditure												
Other (specify) Legal fees				2000								
Dividend payments					3000	3000					4000	
Expenditure subtotal	1420	1460	1370	3670	5530	6410	1890		1540		6720	
Closing bank balance c/fwd	2580	2690	4010	1990	1510	335	1840		4800		1620	

Figure 7.3 Cashflow exercise: answer, part two

▶ Your company may have commissioned a large marketing campaign in the first months of the year, which was not anticipated when drawing up the forecast at the end of the previous year, but which has resulted in increased sales.

▶ There may be some factor in the market which has accelerated the sales the company would have had over, say, the first nine months of the year into the first three months, and particularly into March. If that is the case, identifying it will enable you to recognise that far from being a pattern of increase there will be reduced cash sales in future months.

▶ Your company's products may have become in much greater demand than anticipated and if you can identify that then you might predict considerably increased cash sales in the months ahead.

▶ The company may have made cash sales at the expense of credit sales and, if so, then you should be anticipating reduced income from debtors in the next quarter.

Credit sales

It appears that the company's credit sales in January (payment received in March) were higher than expected: £3,800 as opposed to £2,700. Again, there are several possible explanations:

▶ This may be the case and examination of the sales trends will confirm this.

▶ It may be that some customers, who the company had expected would pay on the usual terms, paid early – in which case you can now *not* expect their payments in future months; your forecast for future months should be reduced.

▶ On the other hand, the company may have made more sales resulting in the increased income, and you might identify that this trend will continue; you can forecast increased funds in the months ahead.

▶ At the beginning of the year the company may have put its credit control staff through special training, given them new incentives, expanded the department. You will have to decide whether the apparent increase in efficiency in collecting the debts (or the efficiency of a similarly trained sales department in making the sales in the first place) will continue or is a temporary effect.

Expenditure for purchases

When you look at the pattern of purchases (higher increases than anticipated towards the later months) you can begin to see that the company may well have made more sales, requiring the purchase of more stocks for sale. On the other hand, the increased pattern of purchases may reflect an inappropriate optimism for the months ahead. Certainly you, as a proactive manager, should be liaising between the sales and purchasing departments to ensure that, for example, the purchases requirements are being based on a proper understanding of the sales and debt collection patterns, and not on a misunderstanding which results in overstocking and over-optimism.

Net wages, NI and PAYE

Given that the company has increased its salaries and wages in the month of March, you should anticipate a small increase in tax and National Insurance outflows in the month of April.

Advertising and promotions

Advertising and promotions are significantly higher than anticipated. As an effective manager, you will want to know whether that was because of a company policy to invest in increased advertising and promotions or whether effective financial control has not been in place in that particular department. In the latter case, effective measures to stop overspending should be implemented with urgency. (In this particular instance, you might find that the increased budget was effectively targeted and has been the reason for the increased sales. However, it is important to examine these factors together *and* separately and not just to assume an intended connection, since it may be coincidental.)

Other expenditure

The company also had an unexpected £2,000 bill for legal fees, which fell due in February. Naturally you will want to know why that has arisen, as it may suggest a future problem – perhaps it was the result of a claim that the company had sold faulty products. In that case you should examine whether or not the company is likely to get more claims and whether or not quality control is effective. You might also want to know why this bill had not been anticipated since in reality the company should have had some forewarning of this type of expenditure; not having processed that into the forecast suggests something may be at fault in the collection or reporting of data in the first place.

It is at this, now fairly advanced, stage in the cashflow budgeting cycle that many managers fail to make the next and most important step. The cashflow forecast should not be regarded as static. All too often, having gone through the process that you have worked through in this chapter, managers will allow their 'actual' columns to fill up along the year and steadily watch an increase in diversity between the forecast and the actual. The important point about cashflow forecasting is that it is a continuous cycle, requiring constant maintenance and updating.

Having processed the result of the first three months, you should use the information gleaned from your analysis of the differences between forecast and actual to completely rewrite the forecast for the twelve months ahead. This should happen periodically, in this case, say, every quarter. For example, you might revise your expectation of cash and credit sales based on your understanding of why there have been significant changes in the March cash inflows and on your understanding of what has been happening in the advertising and promotions department.

In particular, you can see that the company's closing bank balance is not as expected. By the end of the first quarter the closing bank balance is £335, whereas you had forecast a closing bank balance of £1,510. The advantage given by the increase in sales has been more than wiped out by the large legal fees. This may mean that the company will go into overdraft earlier than expected and should contact the bank (or holding company, etc.) and arrange the necessary anticipated finances based on your new information. (Given another set of data you might have found that the company was going to be unexpectedly cash-rich and, rather than waiting until a later date to put funds on deposit, earning high interest, you might transfer some sooner, having reforecast future outflows.)

SOURCES OF DATA

You need data from many sources, particularly in a large company. Indeed the filtering into a master cashflow budget will start at the lowest levels. You can identify immediately that you need data from the following sources (the numbers correspond to the list of data given for the exercise):

▶ (1, 2) the sales force and the sales department, informing you of current and anticipated sales;

▶ (1) the credit control department, informing you of current and anticipated collections from sales. Naturally, as an effective manager, you will want to ensure that data from these two sources is consistent and that the credit control department is receiving accurate and up-to-date information from the sales force. All too often the cash-flow receives an input of data which looks authoritative and useful but is based on two quite separate perceptions by two departments who should be communicating but are not.

▶ (3, 4, 5, 12, 13) the treasury department, to confirm the availability of cash to pay purchases and other commitments;

▶ (7, 8) the purchasing department;

▶ (9) the wages department;

▶ (11) the department dealing with the nominal ledger, i.e. payments of light, heat, telephone and so on (probably again the treasury department);

▶ (14) the advertising and promotions department;

▶ (15, 16) the board, for information relating to proposed capital expenditures, also confirmation of dividend policy.

Last but not least, don't forget you need:

▶ confirmation from the treasury department that the bank account is reconciled, i.e. that the closing bank balance believed to be the case agrees with what the bank believes the company has in its account.

This last point may seem obvious but it is astonishing how many companies do not accurately reconcile their bank account and occasionally find unpleasant surprises. In our experience this can particularly arise when the 'bank' is in fact the company's holding company, both the company and the holding company are doing reconcilations which for one reason or another are not accurately tied up except months down the line, leaving the most important element of cash control completely adrift!

WHEN DO YOU NEED THE DATA?

There must be a reasonable level of accuracy in the data presented or the cashflow forecast will be useless from the point of view of predicting inflows and outflows ahead. On the other hand, the data is needed quickly in order that 'exceptions' can be quickly analysed and appropriate measures taken before a situation is out of date or too far embedded to be rescued. So these management figures must be regarded as 'quick and dirty', i.e. needed quickly and at the sacrifice of some accuracy, but prepared according to sensible predetermined criteria so that not too much accuracy is sacrificed. Whereas you might expect the company's final published accounts – often published months after the year end – to be accurate to within, say, 1%, you might accept an inaccuracy of, say, 5% in your management figures if that will get you the information within days rather than months.

USING THE CASHFLOW

As we've mentioned, the cashflow forecast is useful for reporting your company's needs to the bank and for predicting cash surpluses so as to make the best use of them. There is much more that can be done with the figures. Here is one sequence of events:

▶ A forecast of extra availability of cash, combined with your beliefs about the effectiveness of your increased advertising programme and your new expectation of increased sales resulting from it, will enable you to confirm or extend the budget to the *advertising and promotions department.*

▶ As a result of that, and calculated in tandem with the above, you can discuss the new advertising campaign with the *sales force* in order that they are fully aware of any possible new marketing strategies and the likelihood of increased visibility of the company's products in the marketplace, with the resultant increase in sales.

▶ As a result of that, you can discuss the likelihood of some changed patterns of credit terms with the *credit control department* and possibly revise, upwards or downwards, the expected average debt period for the target for the quarter ahead (see chapter 11).

▶ As a result of that, you will be able to ensure that sufficient funds are available to meet purchasing requirements and you should alert both the purchasing department (*procurement division*) and credit payments section, probably in the *treasury department*, of expected increased outflows.

▶ Based on that, you can anticipate future warehousing requirements (temporary or permanent) and make the appropriate arrangements.

▶ Based on that, and particularly if you make a decision to rent or purchase new warehousing requirements, you can anticipate increased heat, light, telephone, rent, rates, and possibly capital expenditure.

And so on ...

A completely different sequence of events may result, even from the same data, when the data is processed by those who set the overall, 'big-picture', targets for the company. However, this serves as an example of how the data can be extended into useful decision-making criteria.

CASHFLOW VERSUS PROFIT AND LOSS

Profit and loss accounts are budgeted in a very similar way to cashflow. The chart for the year ahead would superficially look very similar. There would, however, be a number of significant differences:

▶ There would be a difference of *timing*. For example, in the profit and loss forecast sales are reported in the month of the sale whereas the cash inflow may be months later. The same applies to purchases, and indeed any bills paid on credit terms.

▶ Income and expenditures are shown *net of VAT* in the profit and loss forecast (as the VAT from sales and purchases is paid over to the government and does not belong to the company) whereas the figures in the cashflow forecast are shown *gross* i.e. including VAT, since that is the amount that will actually come into or go out of the bank. This might appear to distort the figures between the profit and loss and the cashflow but this is corrected by the fact that the cashflow chart also shows the net inflows or outflows directly from or to the VAT office, usually quarterly; this line will not appear in the profit and loss forecast.

▶ The profit and loss forecast will 'spread' *overheads* whereas the cashflow forecast predicts actual payment dates. If, for example, we take the light, heat and telephone expected costs for the year, the cashflow forecast in Figure 7.2 predicts them as £300 in January, £400 in April, £150 in July and £200 in October, as these are the dates when these bills will actually be paid. However, in a profit and loss forecast, the total expected bills for the year, £1,050, would be spread, probably evenly, throughout the year, i.e. £87.50 per month. It might possibly be adjusted for known seasonal fluctuations but would not be adjusted so far as to reflect actual bill payment dates.

▶ As mentioned earlier, *hire purchase payments* will be shown differently: the profit and loss forecast will bear only the monthly interest charge whereas in the cashflow forecast the total amount payable (interest and capital repayment) will be shown.

▶ *Capital expenditure* will not appear in the profit and loss forecast as capital expenditures are not applicable to profit and loss.

► *Dividend payments* (or indeed proprietor's drawings or divisional payments) will not appear in the profit and loss forecast as, again, these are not part of those expenditures.

► The opening and closing *bank balances* will not be shown on the profit and loss forecast as these are irrelevant to profits and losses made during the year.

► *Depreciation*, which is not a flow of actual cash, is an overhead and will be shown in the profit and loss forecast. (See chapter 21 for details of depreciation.)

8

Accounting Ratios and How to Use Them

———◇———

LINDA HAD TO MAKE a financial presentation to thirty key first- and second-line managers. She put up the profit and loss account of the company, and its balance sheet. She explained how the figures of profit looked good, and how stable the company was, given its assets and liabilities. But the questions from the floor came at her hard. Could she prove that the company was selling more profitably? Were any of the company's lines selling worse than others? Could she confirm that cashflows were healthy? Did she know if the company was getting a better or worse return on capital than expected? How had the recent cost-cutting exercises affected the overall profitability? What were the comparisons of results over previous years? Against competitors? Bruised and battered she slunk away to her office and turned to this chapter of Financial Know-how. *If only she'd read it last night!*

THIS CHAPTER sets out a number of commonly used financial ratios which allow you, as a proactive manager, to examine – and explain to others – the success (or otherwise) of your decision-making and the success (or otherwise) of the company as a whole. We stress that it is important that analysis be undertaken (a) over a period of time, (b) against budget and expectations, and (c) by comparison, where possible, with competitors. The crucial factor is the relationship of these ratios to the same ratios calculated in other situations, rather than the one-off figures themselves. Take the published figures of your company and apply ratio analysis to them. It will make the figures come more alive to you, and probably present you with a few surprises – good ones, we hope!

Throughout the chapter we set out the ratios with examples; these will be based on the two simplified financial statements given in Figures 8.1 and 8.2.

GROSS PROFIT PERCENTAGE

This is calculated as follows:

$$\frac{\text{Gross profit}}{\text{Sales income}} \times 100$$

In the Quick Count Ltd example this is:

$$\frac{£4,000}{£12,000} = 33\%$$

This shows the percentage of gross profit earned from direct activity without consideration of administration and overhead costs. In a simple retail situation, gross profit might represent the difference between sales revenue (£12,000) and the purchase costs of the items sold (£8,000). In reality purchase costs may include more, for example: packaging, delivery, some conversion costs (work done to enhance the product prior to sale), etc. In a production company, the direct costs of production may include certain cost allocations and apportionments such as direct production labour, direct production machine-time, and so on. The essential component when calculating gross profit percentage is that the relationship between sales income and cost of sales is where a movement in one is directly reflected by a movement in the other, i.e. if units of items sold were to double then units of items purchased must double also.

Quick Count Ltd			
	Accumulated Depreciation		
	Cost	*Depr.*	*Net*
	£	*£*	*£*
Fixed assets:			
Vehicles and fittings	2000	1000	1000
Patents and trademarks			1000
			2000
Current assets:			
Stocks		1000	
Debtors		500	
Bank and cash		500	
		2000	
Current liabilities:			
Creditors		(200)	
Taxation		(300)	
Proposed dividend		(500)	
		(1000)	
Net current assets			1000
Total assets less current liabilities			3000
Long-term liabilities:			
6% Debentures (secured)			(1000)
Net assets			£2000
Represented by:			
Authorised & issued share capital:			
Ordinary shares of £1			1000
Capital reserve:			
Share premium			200
Revenue reserve:			
Profit & loss balance			800
			£2000

Figure 8.1   *Balance sheet as at 31 March*

Quick Count Ltd		
	£	£
Sales income		12,000
Less: Cost of sales		(8,000)
Gross profit		4,000
Less overheads:		
Selling and distribution		(1,500)
Administration and occupancy		(700)
Directors' salaries		(100)
Depreciation		(440)
Debenture interest		(60)
		(2,800)
Net profit before tax		1,200
Taxation		(300)
Profit after tax		900
Proposed dividend		(500)
Retained earnings this year		400
Balance brought forward from last year		400
Carried forward per balance sheet		£800

Note: Market price per share at the year end is £2.

Figure 8.2 *Profit and loss account for the year ended 31 March*

As with all analysed ratios, there is no right or wrong figure and the resultant percentage, 33% in the example, only has meaning when compared:

(a) historically with gross profit percentages within the company over the past, say, five years;
(b) against expectation, i.e. gross profit percentage forecast;
(c) against the gross profit percentage being achieved by competitors.

Having determined a trend in gross profit percentage, it is then crucial to analyse the trend and learn its lesson. If the ratio is found to be increasing, there may be several reasons why this should be happening:

1 *Improved cost of sales*

The actual volume of sales may be significantly increasing, allowing the company to achieve purchase or manufacturing discounts (economies of large-scale activity), therefore changing the sales/cost relationship. In the Quick Count Ltd example, if sales volume were to multiply tenfold and sales price remained the same, then sales income would go up from £12,000 to £120,000. But where you might expect to pay £80,000 for those items, you might actually obtain a discount of 10% from your suppliers, leaving a cost of £72,000. Gross profit would therefore be £48,000 and the resultant gross profit percentage would be:

$$\frac{£48,000}{£120,000} = 40\%$$

2 *Increased selling price*

The company may have been able to increase its selling price without incurring an increase in purchase price (cost of sales). In the year following these statements, Quick Count Ltd's sales income might be £13,000, while cost of sales remains the same £8,000; this would give a gross profit of £5,000 and the new gross profit percentage would be:

$$\frac{£5,000}{£13,000} = 38.5\%$$

This may be due to one of the company's competitors exiting the market, creating greater demand and therefore pushing up prices. It may be due to technology changes which have made it more important for your customers to buy your particular product rather than the product of one of your competitors; for example, a particular type of computer might have become very popular and may require components your company manufactures whereas a similar component for a different computer may be in less demand if the manufacturers of that computer are not successful in selling their product.

On the other hand, while it may be that your company has won a fight for supremacy of its products, far from being a moment of rejoicing, this may be a moment for caution. If we take the example of the battle, in the early days of video recorders, between VHS, Betamax and '2,000' formats, it is clear that for home domestic use VHS format won the day and therefore manufacturers of VHS-format tapes found their products in considerable demand and could for a short time increase retail prices. However, with such a clear victory established, new manufacturers were able to set up in competition in the reasonable certainty that they were producing for the long term; in the end, retail prices were forced down by keen supply. Anyone analysing their company's trends needs to recognise that if they are in a similar situation, the increase in gross profit percentage may be temporary and they should shortly expect a decrease. Nevertheless, actual revenues may increase, i.e. the volume of money moving may increase even though the gross profit percentage is decreasing.

For most companies, the reality is that the movement in the overall gross profit percentage hides a greater complexity and that complexity, too, must be analysed. Most retailers or manufacturers deal in a variety of products and any meaningful analysis of the trends or comparisons of gross profit percentage should break down into individual gross profit percentages for each product. In a simple example of, say, four products, the components in the Quick Count Ltd example might be as shown in Figure 8.3.

Quick Count Ltd					
	A	**B**	**C**	**D**	**Total**
Sales income	3,000	2,000	5,000	2,000	12,000
Less cost of sales	1,000	3,000	3,000	1,000	8,000
Gross profit	2,000	(1,000)	2,000	1,000	4,000
Gross profit percentage	66%	(50%)	40%	50%	33%

Figure 8.3 *Gross profit percentage, by individual product*

From this you can see that product A produces a gross profit of 66%, product C produces a gross profit of 40%, product D produces a gross profit of 50%. Product B produces a 'gross loss' of 50%, i.e. for every item sold it cost the company 50% more to buy or manufacture it. The following analysis is then important:

▶ Where possible, when analysing individual products, make the same three comparisons as you did for the overall company profits, to discover individual product trends (whether increasing or decreasing) and the reasons behind the trends.

▶ If you had not previously realised that your company was manufacturing a product at a cost greater than its selling price, consider whether simply by stopping producing or selling item B, you immediately increase profitability. In this simple example, by shutting down product B, Quick Count Ltd would now have sales income of a total of £10,000, costs of a total of £5,000 and a resultant total gross profit of £5,000, i.e. an increase in gross profit revenue with a decrease in activity. Presumably they could also release surplus capacity and apply it to a more profitable activity.

▶ On the other hand, you may realise that you have been producing product B at a gross loss; you need to decide whether to continue to do so, to decide if it is still useful as the firm's 'loss leader', i.e. the product which – although it does not make a profit in its own right – is the product which brings customers to *your* company. A 'loss leader' is a deliberate 'hook': for example, you might sell a uniquely sized 'index card' as part of your stationery supply at little or no profit or even at a small loss, knowing that it forces your customers to come back to you for the storage boxes on which you know you make a significant profit. Obviously, it is important to analyse the precise reasons for your particular product mix. In this example, were you to stop supplying the index cards and force your clients to purchase the index cards manufactured by your competitors, you would also lose the resultant profit in what might be your main profitable line – the index card boxes – as your customers would have no need to come to you for those.

This product analysis begins to take you into costing (examined in chapters 13 and 14), where you might consider the merits of 'make or buy' decisions – once you know the direct costs of each product's manufacture you can decide whether it is more economical to produce that product or to engage another supplier to produce it for you.

Remember always that the mere mathematical analysis of gross profit percentage and trends or comparisons is not the end in itself; it is crucial that you examine *the reasons behind* these trends in order to be certain whether they will continue, in which way they will continue to move, and where resources can be targeted to achieve the greatest benefit. Movements in the trend of gross profit percentage must offer information relating to volumes of sales, volumes of purchases, selling price and buying or manufacturing costs. These, in turn, reflect something of whether your company's products are in greater demand or lesser demand and further analysis will enable you to examine why that should be. This leaves you with longer-term planning decisions, i.e. whether to close down certain 'dying' products, whether to boost manufacture of products that are becoming increasingly popular. (Whether, indeed, to have caution in boosting manufacture of products that look as if they are becoming popular when that popularity may be short-term.)

The comparison with the results of your competitors is equally crucial; no matter how well you believe your company is doing because of internal upward trends, you should always be aware that your competitors may have worked out a completely different and superior manufacturing process, or have achieved much more beneficial buying terms from their suppliers which you have failed to seek. By comparing figures with your competitors you can find new avenues of profitability. (Obviously, there is some limit to the degree to which this information is available from competitors; at the extreme end the desire for this information can result in industrial espionage or specifically targeted headhunting!)

NET PROFIT PERCENTAGE

This is calculated as follows:

$$\frac{\text{(pre tax) Net profit}}{\text{Sales income}} \times 100$$

In the Quick Count Ltd example this is:

$$\frac{£1,200}{£12,000} = 10\%$$

Note that net profit is taken 'before tax' rather than 'after tax'. This is because you are examining, as far as possible, the success (or otherwise) of management decisions and financial control within the company; the rate of tax which would affect a net profit calculated 'after tax' is not in the company's control and is therefore eliminated from the calculation.

This is the profit achieved after deduction of all administrative, selling, and other overheads. In addition to movements in the gross profit percentage which will affect the net profit percentage, this ratio will be affected by increases or decreases in overheads. The same considerations relating to gross profit percentage apply also to net profit percentage, i.e. you must compare trends historically, against expectancy, and against competitors' trends; and you need to analyse the components involved in any shift.

Assuming a static gross profit percentage, an increase in net profit percentage suggests lower overhead costs, and a decrease suggests increased overhead costs. To be meaningful, you need to look in detail at the profit and loss account, over several periods.

1 *Volume of activity*

This may have changed. If sales double and cost of sales double (therefore leaving the gross profit percentage the same) it may not follow that overheads are doubled. For example, a factory may be able to double its output within spare capacity and therefore there would be no resultant increase in rent and rates. By the same token, a decrease in activity is probably not going to be reflected by a decrease in all overheads (e.g. rent and rates) so there will be no automatic decrease in net profit percentage.

2 *Individual overheads*

For this ratio to be meaningful, the individual components within the profit and loss account should be examined and even a fairly static trend of net profit percentage may conceal considerable increases and decreases in certain overhead areas, which should be examined. Any one of the components can be calculated as a percentage of sales income, for example selling and distribution. In the Quick Count Ltd example, selling and distribution costs of £1,500 as a percentage of sales income of £12,000 gives a percentage of 12.5%. Were this to change significantly, for example for £12,000 sales income the company spent £3,000 in selling and distribution overheads, management would need to analyse why such a situation should have arisen. You might discover that:

▶ your products are harder to sell because more competitors have entered the field;

▶ your sales force is not so successful and may require retraining in selling techniques, product awareness, or interpersonal skills;

▶ your products are perceived as increasingly out of date;

▶ your distribution costs have increased without your realising that an alternative distribution channel, which was once considered more expensive, could now be considered more economical. (Ratio analysis often allows you to examine alternatives to a policy of 'do today as we did yesterday'.)

Similarly, any other movement in the overheads should be analysed in depth to examine what is causing the movement and to determine whether this is a positive or negative trend, a long-term or short-term trend, a trend to be encouraged or fought against, and so on.

CURRENT ASSET TURNOVER

This is calculated as follows:

$$\frac{\text{Cost of sales + overheads}}{\text{Average current assets}}$$

In the Quick Count Ltd example this is:

$$\frac{£8,000 + £2,800}{£2,000} = 5.4 : 1$$

(assuming the figure for current assets is identical at each year end).

(N.B. In this context, 'average' means opening current assets plus closing current assets, divided by 2.)

This means that current assets were used 5.4 times during the year to pay the costs of the company's activities.

You have to balance the desirability of having sufficient liquid funds to pay the company's way on a day-to-day basis against tying up too much in liquid funds and not planning for the long term through capital investment. The most important use of this ratio is in comparison with expectation, i.e. in the company's long-term plans it will expect a certain ratio, leaving free other monies for longer-term investment; if the true ratio is at variance from expectation then the reasons should be analysed, particularly to determine whether it is that management has used assets poorly or that the assets that were expected to be available are simply not there.

WORKING CAPITAL TO TURNOVER

This is calculated as follows:

$$\frac{\text{Sales income (Turnover)}}{\text{Net current assets}}$$

In the Quick Count Ltd example this is:

$$\frac{12,000}{1,000} = 12 : 1$$

This shows the number of £s in sales that the company obtained for each £1 of its working capital.

Clearly the company seeks to maximise the number of £s it can produce in sales revenues for every £1 of working capital investment. This is achieved both by increasing sales and controlling working capital. (See chapter 9.)

WORKING CAPITAL TO TOTAL ASSETS

This is calculated as follows:

$$\frac{\text{Working capital}}{\text{Total assets (Fixed and Current assets)}} \times 100$$

In the Quick Count Ltd example this is:

$$\frac{£1,000}{£4,000} = 25\%$$

This shows the relative liquidity of total assets and distribution of resources. It indicates the degree to which available resources have been applied to the more immediate short term (the working capital) as opposed to longer-term investments including fixed assets which provide the bedrock for longer-term future trading.

The use of this analysis is against expectation; the company will have a long-term investment programme and will seek to draw from its profits sufficient monies for long-term investment. This ratio shows the degree to which the long-term investment programme is being applied successfully. Actual results will be measured against the company's anticipation.

GEARING

Gearing examines the overall financing of the company and shows the relationship between fixed-interest financing and equity financing.

This is calculated as follows:

$$\frac{\text{Fixed-interest loans}}{\text{Ordinary shares}}$$

In the Quick Count Ltd example this is:

$$\frac{£1,000}{£1,000} = 1 : 1$$

Cumulative preference shares (i.e. preference shares which guarantee a dividend at some time prior to the availability of dividends to the equity shareholders) may be included under fixed-interest loans in some calculations; similarly, non-cumulative preference shares – on which if the dividend is not paid in a given year it is lost – may be included under ordinary shares in some calculations. Clearly, the important point is to examine 'like for like' and ensure that the same criteria are applied to any comparisons historically, against expectancy, or against competition.

A company which has a high percentage of fixed-interest loans may be vulnerable in that it has to meet its interest commitments whether the profits are there or not and could therefore be forced into short-term measures – sales of capital assets and so on – whereas a company with a higher percentage of equity funding is less vulnerable as it does not have to pay a dividend if it does not have the funds to do so. (In the long term, a company which does not pay dividends may find its share values decreasing and its perceived worth very low.)

In the event of changing trends, the company, and external financial analysts, will be looking to see why the gearing has changed. For example, there may be a move towards increased fixed-interest loans because the company is unable to attract equity investments; conversely, the company may be seeking equity investment because it is unable to obtain further support from its bankers or the financial institutions. In any event, the background reason for the position the company finds itself in and for the decisions it is being forced to take should be examined, and management should apply itself to corrective measures. Sometimes a practical move is needed: the company may have to invest in new technologies to attract either form of support; sometimes it simply has to correct investors' perception: it has not made itself attractive to would-be investors by failing to market itself successfully or explain its long-term plans clearly.

RETURN ON AVERAGE CAPITAL EMPLOYED (ROACE)

This is calculated as follows:

$$\frac{\text{Net profit (after tax)}}{\text{Capital + Reserves}} \times 100$$

In the Quick Count Ltd example this is:

$$\frac{£900}{£2,000} \times 100 = 45\%$$

Profit is taken after tax (net) as this is the figure available for return to shareholders, at least in theory. In the case of the Quick Count Ltd example a figure of 45% (a somewhat high figure for the sake of example) would almost certainly indicate both successful long-term growth and high profit margins.

The ROACE figure represents the percentage earned by the owners' (shareholders) investment in their company.

Obviously, they desire as high a rate of return as possible.

During the recent recession, it was a sad fact of life that, even for companies that survived the recession, the ROACE for many small businesses (1% or 2%, break-even or even 1% or 2% loss, requiring further personal risk or investment) was such that many owners of small businesses would literally have been financially better off – at least in the short term – by closing their companies down, investing the money in a reasonable building society account and watching television for a year! Of course, many personal, political and social factors, and longer-term expectations, play a part in the actual decision; but, if nothing else, this analysis showed the vulnerability of many small businesses operating at very low net profit margins with low return, no return or negative return on capital employed. For small businesses, this can come about through even small imbalances in the commercial world, let alone the imbalances evident during recessions.

9

Working Capital Control

———◇———

EVERY NON-FINANCIAL manager must know how their department fits into the working capital equation; i.e. what they contribute to day-to-day money coming in, and what they need for day-to-day expenditure. If, for example, you are the working capital controller of a company, your job is to manage the short-term assets and liabilities in such a way that they make a positive contribution to the daily flow of cash (see chapter 7). For example, it is obviously in the company's interest to collect the debts as quickly as possible.

THE LONG-TERM survival of a company is often dependent on its strategic policy of long-term investment in fixed assets: principally its plant, machinery and technology. However, companies don't survive long term if they neglect the needs of the short and medium term. To survive in the present, a company needs cash: to pay wages, to buy stocks, to pay the phone and electricity bills, and so on. The essence of this survival is control of working capital, now recognised by many of the country's leading companies as the major area of managerial – financial – focus, and the basis of effective cash control. Companies that ignore working capital requirements can suffer short-term difficulties which, in extreme cases, can thwart long-term planning and even lead to corporate collapse.

Working capital is basically the current assets (stocks, debtors, short-term investments, cash) less current liabilities (creditors, taxes, dividends, etc.). A company must control its working capital, keeping the right balance of funds on hand to meet day-to-day requirements. Some larger companies employ a Working Capital Controller for this purpose.

Ratio analysis (the subject of chapter 8) provides you with a number of tools for working capital control. For this chapter, let's refer again to the two financial statements of Quick Count Ltd (pages 78 and 79).

DEBT COLLECTION PERIOD

This is calculated as follows:

$$\frac{\text{Trade debtors}}{\text{Credit sales}} \times 12 \text{ or } 52 \text{ or } 365$$

In the Quick Count Ltd example, assuming all sales are on credit, this is:

$$\frac{500}{12,000} \times \frac{365 \text{ (days)}}{1} = 15.21 \text{ days}$$

This means that debtors represent (on average) the last 15 days' sales.

Debt collection period can be set as a target for staff in the debt collection department. Clearly, the lower the figure the better, for a number of reasons:

1 Debtors, i.e. people who owe you money, represent a loan from your company to your customers' companies, probably at no interest, while depriving you of interest-earning investment.

2 The longer a debt is outstanding, the greater the increase in risk of non-payment and the greater your company's vulnerability to suffering liquidity problems.

3 The more money tied up in debtors, the less there is available for purchasing more items for sale, and therefore

possibly the fewer opportunities you have for increasing turnover.

Having set a target, management must ensure that variances from that target are examined. An increasing number of days may represent an inefficiency on the part of debt collection staff, which should be addressed. However, more complex factors may be involved, reflecting the perennial conflict between the sales force and those responsible for debt collection:

▶ The sales force will generally want to sell to anybody (and probably therefore increase their personal commissions), whereas the debt collection staff are concerned that the sale be turned into cash. An increasing number of days' debt collection period may mean that the sales force is selling more product, but to less reliable customers, or that they are negotiating unacceptably generous terms in order to make extra sales.

▶ It may mean that your sales force is unable to sell to the usual customers and is having to find new markets which are either less reliable or negotiating tighter deals for themselves. Either of these two possibilities may reflect the quality, or perceived quality, of your products. They suggest that your products are becoming less marketable or that your competitors have promoted their products more effectively than you are doing; this suggests a need to examine, initially, the work of the marketing and advertising departments.

There can be positive reasons why the debt collection period may increase. For example, your sales force may have negotiated very large quantities of sales which are highly profitable but in return for which they have negotiated extended credit terms.

As with all ratios, it is the analysis of the reasons behind movements which is important, particularly for longer-term planning.

CREDIT PAYMENT PERIOD

This is calculated as follows:

$$\frac{\text{Trade creditors}}{\text{Credit purchases}} \times 12 \text{ or } 52 \text{ or } 365$$

In the Quick Count Ltd example, assuming all purchases ('cost of sales') are on credit, this is:

$$\frac{200}{8,000} \times 365 \text{ (days)} = 9.12 \text{ days}$$

This means that creditors represent (on average) the last 9 days' purchases.

Clearly there is something to be said for the target for this figure to be as high as possible, i.e. that you should be extending the credit you take from your suppliers as much as possible in order to be receiving from them, effectively, an interest-free loan. However, you must consider not antagonising suppliers who might subsequently negotiate tighter terms or, in certain circumstances, refuse to supply except on terms of 'cash with order'. Furthermore, your suppliers' companies may consider that the reason you are extending credit is not because you are unwilling to pay but rather that you are unable to pay – and they may become concerned over extending further credit. Your sending out the wrong signals may create difficulties in the longer term. Certainly, companies that do face financial difficulties often first manifest this by extending the delay in payments to suppliers.

It is worth noting that very large companies often use their 'clout' to deliberately extend their credit payment period, particularly to smaller companies supplying them; some companies are notorious for using their muscle in 'take it or leave it' deals, often to the point of pushing suppliers to the wall, knowing that there will be others ready to take their place. Any manager of a smaller company faced with the possibility of supplying large companies and therefore almost certainly tying up a significant percentage of the business's available working capital, should consider the vulnerability that such a decision would produce. At the time of writing, proposals are being offered (by both major UK political parties, to woo the votes represented by small businesses) to force companies to pay debts or face automatic, statutory, interest charges for delayed payment. The policies that may be adopted, and their effect, remain to be seen.

WORKING CAPITAL RATIO

This is calculated as follows:

$$\frac{\text{Current assets}}{\text{Current liabilities}}$$

In the Quick Count Ltd example this is:

$$\frac{£2,000}{£1,000} = 2 : 1$$

Current assets includes stock on the basis that in the normal course of trade stock will be sold and realised into cash.

Too high a figure (e.g. 3.1) might show a poor use of liquid assets and the effective financial manager – or Working Capital Controller – might seek to commit some of the excess working capital to longer-term planning, through capital commitment or investment, but only as part of an overall long-term strategy decision.

A deterioration in the ratio might show that the company is having increasing difficulties meeting its day-to-day running costs. If this is recognised by suppliers it is highly likely that lines of credit will be cut off and the company will be forced to accept emergency measures such as paying cash with order.

LIQUIDITY RATIO

This is calculated as follows:

$$\frac{\text{Debtors + Cash (+ any other short-term assets)}}{\text{Current liabilities}}$$

Known also as the 'acid test' or 'quick' ratio, the liquidity ratio examines a company's ability to pay its immediate debts, i.e. to use its current assets to pay instant demands. The top line represents current assets less stocks – clearly, for this purpose current assets cannot include stocks as stocks cannot so quickly be turned into cash, having usually to go through the process of sale and then debt collection.

Given that the reality of commercial life is that a company does not, in the usual course of business, face a demand for instant payment from all its creditors, 1:1 as given in the example is arguably a poor use of liquid cash and a figure of something like 0.7:1 is often considered acceptable. This is equivalent to a bank branch holding just a small percentage of the money represented by its customers' bank balances, on the basis that there is virtually no likelihood of all the customers wanting their money out on the same day.

PREDICTING BANKRUPTCY

One important use of examining the trend in both the working capital ratio and the liquidity ratio is in predicting bankruptcy. For this purpose, the liquidity ratio has been shown to be the most accurate predictor. A study in 1966 took 79 companies that had failed or were unable to meet their financial commitments and paired them with companies within the same industries that had not failed. It then analysed the failed companies over a period of five years prior to the collapse and examined equivalent periods for their paired companies. It used over thirty conventional ratios, including the liquidity ratio and working capital ratio.

The liquidity ratio was the most successful predictor of bankruptcy, with only 10% of companies wrongly classified in the year prior to failure and 22% in the five years prior. The working capital ratio was not so successful: 20% of companies were wrongly classified in the year prior to failure and 31% in the five years prior.

WAYS TO IMPROVE WORKING CAPITAL

Working capital control is always important, of course, but especially so when the predictions of ratio analysis and stock control (see chapter 10) suggest difficulties in the months ahead. In that case, the management's basic goal is very simple: to increase net cash inflows, so that it can increase net cash balances at the bank or on deposit, or decrease the overdraft. There are several ways of improving working capital:

▶ Reduce stockholding, making alternative arrangements with suppliers and, possibly, arranging new internal procedures to speed up the flow of goods from 'goods inwards', through warehousing and onto the production floor. (But also see chapter 10.)

▶ Offer incentives for early debt payment. It may be worthwhile offering a small discount for early settlement of invoices. To determine if this is economically viable, consider the additional interest that will be earned by having the money in the bank earlier, plus a possible reduction on overdraft or loan fees for the period, against the discount given.

▶ Encourage the sales force to promote earlier payment, with incentives, both at the time of sale and at the contract-signing stage.

▶ Negotiate with your suppliers to gain more favourable credit terms for payment of invoices, either increasing the amount of time allowed before payment is due or negotiating a discount for earlier payment.

▶ Ensure that overheads are as economically controlled as possible. With the privatised markets for utilities, competitive buying is available and there are even cost-management consultants who can advise on the most economical suppliers for heat, light, telephone, water, and so on.

▶ For the short term, consider those areas of cost that can be reduced or deferred without affecting the short-term running of the company. In particular, consider advertising and promotion, training, marketing, and so on. But beware of falling into the trap of believing that these are not necessary overheads. Companies are like car engines: they not only need regular supplies of petrol in order to run but they also need regular servicing if they are not to break down. Plumbers insist that they make more money putting right the efforts of do-it-yourself enthusiasts than they do on jobs where they are called in from the start; the cash investment needed to restart training and marketing, for example, is often far higher than the amount saved by restricting these activities for too long.

▶ 'Make or buy' decisions: consider the cost of producing, in-house, certain goods or services, or certain stages of production, compared to the cost of outsourcing that work to other companies who, being specialists, may be able to sell you the same product or service more cheaply. Many companies are now outsourcing the work of whole departments that they used to operate internally, with just one internal manager interfacing with the contracted company or companies. This has had the effect of bringing companies back to what is called their 'core business'.

▶ 'Lease or buy' decisions: consider whether to invest large sums of capital into purchasing capital equipment, buildings, and so on, or whether to take leases in order to obtain the same equipment.

▶ Consider sources of finance for particular projects: whether to take out a loan and over what period, and whether to seek further investment through, say, share capital from investors.

▶ There are other specialist sources of short-term finance such as factoring, debts and so on (see chapter 17).

While the goal (rather simplistically stated) of increasing net inflows and balances on deposit is a sensible one, it should not be considered in isolation. As an effective manager, you should calculate a balance between the pure finance and the non-financial effects, such as the antagonism caused by your delaying payment to creditors, particularly without agreement; as mentioned earlier, your creditors' reaction could simply create a potential cashflow crisis for the company rather than a solution. If finance can be regarded as the company's blood supply (as suggested in chapter 2) then, just as a doctor can tell a lot by examining the blood, so you can tell a lot by examining the management of working capital around your company – but it is wise to remember that there are plenty of other ailments to be guarded against.

10

Stock Control

———◇———

'*FOR THE WANT of a nail the shoe was lost; for the want of a shoe the horse was lost; for the want of a horse the rider was lost; for the want of a message the war was lost; and all for the want of a horseshoe nail.*' *This is a story of bad stock control in the horseshoe nail department. Stock is expensive to hold: it ties up money to buy it, money to maintain it in good condition, money to house it, and money to secure it from theft or damage. Every manager must look at their stock requirements with the goal of reducing stockholding to the minimum commensurate with efficiency.*

ASK AN operations director of a manufacturing company, or a retail organisation, what is one of the biggest headaches and somewhere at the top of the list will be stock and stock control. Ask any first-line manager in warehousing, distribution or retailing, and the answer will be the same: stock and stock control. The difference willl be that in the first case the problem is too much stock and in the second case too little stock.

You should consider the following three questions when examining your company's stockholding policy:

1. When does stock get sold?

This question, put to delegates on financial courses, produces a wide variety of answers: 'When the goods move out of the warehouse'; 'When the invoice is raised'; 'When the invoice is paid;' etc., etc. It is partly a trick question: the answer which shows the greatest awareness is 'Never'.

Stock is never sold!

Of course, individual items on the shelves are sold but if you were to walk into your warehouse every day of the year and take a photograph there would always be some stock 'on the shelves' and to that extent there is a hardcore of stock which is 'never sold'. This represents cash tied up in stocks instead of sitting in your bank earning interest. Conversely, your suppliers have released their stocks from their warehouses, replacing it with your money in their bank earning interest for them.

This is the basis of 'Just in Time' stockholding, which gets its name from stock replacement 'just in time', i.e. when the last item in the warehouse goes out of the door a new delivery comes in moments later 'just in time' to fill the shelves again. In a totally predictable, clockwork, world there would never be any items of stock on any shelves anywhere.

Lower stockholding also brings with it the additional benefits of lower warehousing costs, lower security staff costs, lower costs of stock maintenance, lower risk of theft or accidental damage, lower insurance costs, and so on.

Costs of stockholding are dramatically demonstrated in the following story. We spoke to the owner of a large picture library which supplies images to the film, television and magazine companies. So that they have a choice, these companies will often call for, say, twenty images from which they might select one; but for a period of time they hold all twenty pictures at their premises. The owner told us he would need a building literally twice the size of the one he successfully operates from if he were to have to hold all of his pictures. In fact, he said, his greatest nightmare was that one morning all the images out on loan would be returned in one go!

2. How much stock should you have?

Clearly, the world is not totally predictable and mechanistic. You cannot be absolutely certain when each of your customers will ask you to supply them with an item, nor can you be absolutely certain that your suppliers can supply exactly when requested. The stock you should therefore hold (apart from the vague and possibly unhelpful term 'minimum') is the quantity of stock you would expect to sell, on average, within your normal ordering cycle. If you order once a month, you should order sufficient for one month's average demand (also taking into account any seasonal or cyclical trends). Added to that should be a 'buffer' (also minimal) representing your security over unexpected demands or unexpected let-downs in supply by your suppliers.

3.   When should you re-order?

This then becomes a factor of the previous two questions. Your re-ordering is based on your relationship with your suppliers. At a very simple level, if you expect a delivery on the first day of every month and your quantity of stockholding is geared to that delivery (i.e. on the first day of each month your suppliers deliver sufficient stock for the month ahead), then re-ordering must take place within the previous month, giving your suppliers time to deliver on the first. If your suppliers take one week to process and deliver an order, you need to order one week prior to the first of the month.

On the other hand, you can become slightly more sophisticated by recognising that demand by your customers will not be totally regular and therefore you will need to order from your suppliers at different and unpredictable times. For their part, your suppliers still take one week to deliver from the time you re-order. What you must therefore do is calculate the average amount of stock you should be holding during the time between placing the order and receiving the new delivery, and your re-order 'flag' should be set to that level of stock, whenever you reach it. This can most easily be seen with the example of books on the bookshelves of large retail book suppliers in the high street. There may be, say, eight copies of a particular book stacked facing outwards on the shelf, and on average that stock would last for approximately one month, therefore on average the shop is selling approximately two per week. If they know that their suppliers take one week to supply them, a flag (often a simple coloured card) is placed after the sixth book, alerting them to the fact that they now have approximately one week's supply left. This is the 'trigger' for them to re-order, because, on average, 'just in time' the new consignment of books should arrive. The shop staff will regularly parade the shop looking for flags that have been exposed or the flag may even have a message in bold lettering asking the customer purchasing the sixth book to take the flag to the counter with them. 'Intelligent' tills at the checkouts of Asda, Tesco, and other large supermarkets, instigate an automatic stock replenishment process (known as 'auto-rep').

'Just in Time' stockholding, created in Japan, has had the effect of taking stocks out of warehouses and putting them on the roads, increasing the stock haulage business considerably. If a company needs to restock an average 100 products each week and has an average delivery lead-time of two weeks, at any given moment its lorries will be carrying average stock of 200 items.

The goal is to achieve the maximum sales for the lowest stockholding, which equates to the highest turnover figure (see computation below).

STOCK TURNOVER

This is calculated as follows:

$$\frac{\text{Cost of sales}}{\text{Average stock}}$$

Looking back at the financial statements of Quick Count Ltd, in their example this is:

$$\frac{£8,000}{£1,000} = 8 \text{ times}$$

(This assumes £1,000 in stock at each year end.)

What this means is that during the year total stock is used and replaced 8 times. Note that it is the average stock which is important. Were you to look at two annual balance sheets, showing the opening stock to have been £2,000 and the closing stock £1,000, then the average stockholding would have been £1,500 and stock turnover would have been:

$$\frac{£8,000}{£1,500} = 5.33 \text{ times}$$

i.e. stock is used and replaced 5.33 times during the year.

A high or increasing stock turnover is generally a healthy sign.

As a proactive manager, you will consider getting suppliers to hold stock for you, which you will call off 'as needed'. This transfers the costs of stockholding to your suppliers. Since this is not in their interests, you may then be able to negotiate considerable discounts to take stock earlier, which may be economical. Armed with these figures, you will at least have some useful bargaining chips when negotiating prices to be paid for purchases.

OTHER STOCKHOLDING CONSIDERATIONS

Increasing stocks

While the ratio above examines stockholding from the point of view of absolute minimum stockholding, there are reasons why you might, on the other hand, increase your stockholding (other than to maintain buffer stocks while re-ordering, anticipate unexpected demands from customers, or pre-empt any unreliability of your suppliers). You might buy large quantities of stocks in the following circumstances:

▶ if you know that suppliers are going out of business and you want to secure a long-term future position while either negotiating with new manufacturers or considering your own manufacturing capabilities;

▶ if stocks are available at such an incredibly cheap rate that the disadvantage of having less money in the bank and the cost of maintaining the stocks are outweighed by the discounts received; this could arise in buying liquidation stocks from a company that has failed or because the company is rationalising its own stockholding and is prepared to sell very cheaply in order to discard a costly warehouse. You might find taking on such warehousing costs economical;

▶ if your suppliers, while not unreliable themselves, are subject to unreliability in their own supply – for example, certain commodities are subject to the vagaries of climate and when there is a supply available it is wise to buy in bulk rather than risk being unable to buy at another time because of crop failure.

The proactive manager must consider – and balance – all the points in this chapter when examining stockholding. Remember, however, that whatever the considerations which go into your eventual decision, your overall goal is always that of minimum stockholding in the given circumstances. Many older companies have converted some of their warehouses into offices, their old practice of keeping masses of stock now largely a thing of the past.

Maintaining adequate stocks

Different companies have *different stockholding costs*. As a proactive manager, you should ensure that you know the stockholding costs – and thereby the consequences of overstocking – in your company. But balance against that the risk factor: what would be the cost of being out of stock? and for how long?

There is a rough rule of thumb across industry – which you must calculate more specifically for your particular field – that the annual cost of holding an item in stock is about 25% of the item's value – or about 2% per month.

Different industry sectors have different 'norms' for *stock losses*. Losses can arise if your goods are perishable, from theft, deterioration, and so on. Dixons' norm will be X% while M & S's norm will be Y%. In assessing your stock-holding costs you need to be aware of those norms, and ensure that you are not losing an unacceptable amount.

You should consider the best practices of *stock consolidation*. This is the ability to condense items from different locations into, say, a new shop rather than increasing overall stock levels. When a chain of jewellers opens a new branch it can often initially stock that new outlet by collecting items from around the chain. The new outlet then makes the money to restock itself and replenish the other branches, meaning that cashflows are not overly strained.

Reducing stocks

Opportunities to initiate stock reductions often arise within companies that do not have efficient stock ordering and holding procedures. Management will often try to hide mistakes and stocks that will probably never be sold sit in the warehouse because no one has the courage to admit they should never have been ordered in the first place. These can be the first to go.

Be aware of the probable responses of others to changes in stockholding policies, particularly when reducing stock. When management embark upon reductions in stock, first-line managers tend to build up little 'ammunition' dumps around the site like Rommel in the African desert positioning fuel dumps!

Fashion and technology lead to changes in demand. The proactive manager should make regular provision for obsolete, damaged and slow-moving stock.

11

Credit Control

—◇—

THE COMPANY received a summons for non-payment of debt from a supplier, Ajax Components Ltd. It checked its records and agreed that it owed the money, which it paid. But Ajax Components had not sent out statements or reminders, and in fact had no formal system of credit control. The result was conflict, and the company sought a new supplier.

Customers are hard to get and easy to lose. Effective credit control is designed to minimise the friction and ensure that working capital, from the collection of debts, is properly maintained. Once a customer is won, it is important that procedures allow for the maintenance of a healthy relationship between companies, which respects the needs of both parties. Ajax Components lost a valuable customer, simply because of poor credit control.

D EBTS ARISE because you – through your company – give credit to the people who buy from you. You encourage them to buy now and pay later. Unfortunately, sometimes your customers buy now and cannot afford to pay later. Avoiding that problem, or at least controlling its extent, is the basis of an efficient and planned credit control policy. The system must be flexible enough to meet changing needs from time to time; for example, if you are satisfied that a good customer has a short-term cashflow problem you might extend extra credit – but you would plan for this carefully. Many of the most common problems can be avoided by planning.

Most delayed payments and bad debts do not arise because your customers are short of cash. Most arise because of bad organisation on their part and lack of control on your part.

Customers who have an organised system for payments are rarely a problem unless they really do have a cashflow crisis. In the main, they will enter your invoice into their purchase ledger system with a predetermined pay date, and it will be paid on that date. You may be able to affect that date by stating, on your invoice, the acceptable payment time (e.g. 'payable 30 days after receipt'). The arrangement you want to make with each other should be clearly set out from the beginning when supply is being negotiated.

It is the customers with no particular system that are the problem. Generally speaking, an invoice, when it arrives on that customer's desk, has a certain priority based on their relationship with you. The customer has a mental note, at least, of when that invoice will be paid. But the list of circumstances that can delay that payment are legion:

▶ tardiness: invoices left in an in-tray and ignored because of pressure of work;

▶ fire-fighting: your customer only pays creditors who phone up and demand payment ('the squeaky hinge gets the oil');

▶ priority by need: invoices are paid as and when the customer needs to re-order from that supplier;

▶ complacency: your customer gets to know who makes a fuss and who doesn't, and pays the one who will moan if ignored;

▶ experience: if your customer comes to realise that you are so inefficient you will be unaware that they haven't paid for some time, then they will take advantage of that situation.

By being a creditor who doesn't get paid, you create a number of difficulties for yourself:

▶ You suffer cashflow problems of your own because money

you have earned is not in your bank, it's in someone else's. If you have an overdraft, you are paying interest to finance that overdraft in order to give someone else an interest-free loan.

▶ Your customer may, at any time, collapse for financial or other reasons. The longer your customer owes you money, the longer you are rolling the dice on the gamble that when it happens, yours is one of the debts that gets paid. Getting your money out as soon as possible reduces the risk.

▶ Ironically, given your generosity as a creditor, the less your customer sees your name, the less business you might do. If one of your competitors chases for cash efficiently then their name is well known to the customer and when re-ordering comes around it will be that name – not your name – that is on the tip of their tongue. Even more ironically, you only increase the chances of getting an order over the head of that more visible competitor when the customer knows there are cashflow problems ahead and you are the soft touch that might get them past it. If you get orders only when times are rough, you are increasing the risk of being the debt that goes 'bust'.

The solution to these situations is to be systematic from the outset and apply a few simple rules.

Send out clear invoices

Apart from legal requirements (which will be decided by your company) and terms and conditions of supply, it's important to show the following information on your invoices:

▶ details of the goods or services supplied, and date of supply;

▶ any contact names, order references, etc.;

▶ amount charged with a clear figure showing the amount payable. This is particularly true if there are complex discounts or early-payment incentives; if you make it difficult for your customer to see what to pay then your invoice goes in an in-tray that guarantees a delay of some sort;

▶ the date on which payment is demanded;

▶ the address to which payment is to be made;

▶ a full telephone number (including the STD code and international code if to overseas customers) so that queries can be addressed easily.

In addition, these are some features of efficient invoicing:

▶ make invoices at least A4 in size, anything else gets lost in the 'pile';

▶ consider 'special effects' – one of our clients was convinced his credit control was enhanced by his using fluorescent pink invoices and statements. ('They never miss one of my invoices,' he said, 'in fact they pay them so they can file them – it's easier on their eyes!')

▶ give a remittance advice (perhaps a tear-off slip or 'two page set') so that your customer does not have to write a letter enclosing settlement;

▶ be efficient: send out the invoice promptly, giving the signal that you are on the ball, and will be following up late payment equally promptly.

At the present time, remember that if you want to charge interest, you must set out the terms from the outset. You cannot just impose interest for late payment if you have not indicated that it is your policy to do so.

Have a statement policy

Some companies do not issue statements, some regularly do. Make your mind up on your policy and get your customer used to it. If you do intend to use statements, make sure that you have a statement run on a fixed, pre-planned date. We would suggest every month-end. Show clearly what invoices are overdue and by how long. You might consider attaching copies of the outstanding invoices to the statements. Make clear how much is demanded. Have a section on the statement where you can 'personalise' demand messages; it will tell your customer that the statement run is not just a computerised procedure but one in which you have taken an active interest.

Be alert

Your credit control department should understand that invoicing and statements are important and to be dealt with promptly. Debt-chasing should be 'keen'. The day following an overdue payment, they should be telephoning the customer to chase for payment. Any threats of action to be taken should be followed through promptly.

Within the department, use the following two tools as both monitors and targets for your own staff:

The debtor summary

This is a most important tool for monitoring and controlling debts (and thereby cashflow). It will tell you who owes you money, how much they owe, and how long they have owed it. In circumstances where you have earlier decided to take additional risks, it will tell you the degree to which normal credit terms have been extended.

This document should not be used like a fireworks display, a spectacle to watch with amazement. Use it as a working tool. If certain debts become older than planned for, take action. Ensure that, if your summary is computerised, there is an exception 'flag' which will notify you when certain parameters have been broken, i.e. too much debt, too long in paying, etc.

Average debt outstanding

A further important tool you can use to monitor your debtors, and for that matter your credit control department, is the average debt period. Calculating the average of all your debts and how long they have been outstanding produces a measure of overall efficiency in debt collection. For example, you make sales, on average, of £28,000 per month, which would be £336,000 per annum. You discover that your debtors at a certain month-end are £41,500. The calculation of average debt outstanding at that point in time is:

$$\frac{£41,500}{£336,000} \times 365 = 45.08 \text{ days}$$

It can also be worked out in weeks:

$$\frac{£41,500}{£336,000} \times 52 = 6.42 \text{ weeks}$$

or months:

$$\frac{£41,500}{£336,000} \times 12 = 1.48 \text{ months}$$

All the answers are effectively the same, of course. They mean that your average debt outstanding at that point in time is around one and a half months' worth of sales. That measure is not, by itself, of much use; you would need to know what was either normal, or appropriate. One test is to monitor the progress of the period. If the average period is getting longer, the period of collection is getting longer. In short, you are collecting less efficiently, probably causing cashflow difficulties and taking increased risks. Another test is to have a target period to aim for. Any time your average debt outstanding exceeds the target period, you must investigate why.

In particular, the warning sign is if the percentage is increasing. In that case it suggests either:

▶ the credit control dept is becoming less efficient (suggesting that your procedures are being ignored); or

▶ the sales force is selling to less reliable customers (suggesting that your traditional customers may have gone elsewhere, your products are not as well thought of as they used to be, competition has become more fierce, and so on).

Never mind the width, feel the quality

A small number of customers probably account for a large percentage of debt outstanding. Ensure that you target your efforts and resources at recovering the debts that make the most overall difference. It may feel like a victory to get a £5 debt owed from a year ago, but if that means you have lost recovery of a £5,000 debt owed for two months, you have not achieved anything of value. Worse, in the time it takes you to realise that the larger debts is unpaid, your company may get into financial difficulty and collapse. You could probably have avoided that by monitoring those debts that make an impact.

Bear in mind also that debt collection takes time. Don't put any resources into chasing after debts so small that they are literally not worth the effort. And don't get into that position by offering credit on too small an amount, where everyone knows that debt-chasing would be pointless. In those cases insist on cash with order.

When taking risks, set the safety net

To ensure that bad debts stay at a reasonable level, one caution is to allow customers only a responsible amount of credit. The more risky you believe a customer to be, the less credit you should extend to that business – if at all. The actual amounts involved are a factor of circumstance: the size of your business, the costs of your individual products, the frequency of purchases by that customer, the field in which you work, the size of 'normal' orders by other customers, and so on. There are credit check companies that can offer reports on company viability; but remember that these are often based on accounts filed at Companies House and they can be up to ten months out of date.

PLAYING IN THE BIG PLAYGROUND

Larger companies use their 'muscle' to force their suppliers to extend longer-than-usual periods of credit to them. If you want to supply them, you have to take their terms. They use you, and others like you, as a free source of finance. If you want to play in this big playground, you may not be able to avoid this harsh reality, but you should at least be aware of the rules before you get into the game. Legislation to force companies to pay statutory interest on delayed payments – created specifically to protect small businesses from this big-business clout – may have some effect if properly policed. The problem is, however, that companies are not breaking their agreements; they are forcing people to make unreasonable agreements. And it's unlikely that that can be effectively legislated against.

Dealing with large companies is a two-edged sword:

Pros

► they take large orders;

► they are probably less risky in the long run;

► you have less administration dealing with one large company than ten small ones.

Cons

▶ delayed payments can force your company to find other finance to meet the credit given;

▶ the large orders need to be either purchased in or manufactured: more strain on your cashflow;

▶ you are often at their beck and call, and can risk neglecting and alienating other customers in order to meet their demands;

▶ large companies will demand preferential rates; you may be working for very reduced margins, increasing your risks;

▶ competitors seeking to serve that large client may undercut you, or force you to squeeze already tight margins.

AND NOW THE GOOD NEWS

Believe it or not, bad debts are a healthy sign in a company. They show that the company is taking risks, and no company survives long in a competitive, dynamic environment if it doesn't take risks. A percentage of risks are bound to fail; that is why they are called risks. However, if that percentage is too high, profits can quickly turn to losses.

12

Cost-Cutting Exercises

———◇———

COST-CUTTING is a responsibility of all managers. You make the day-to-day decisions that can limit waste, prevent the unnecessary tying-up of funds, and contribute continually to the best use of assets. Every non-financial manager has an obligation to ensure that they know where every pound is being spent, why, and what alternatives are available. The tools of cost-cutting analysis and planning in this chapter will help you to examine your department in this light.

COMPETITION, internally from within the UK, and – more important – external both from established economies such as the USA and other European Union countries and, now, from the so-called emerging countries, has led to a drive for ever-increasing productivity. Productivity is about making the best use of people, systems and capital. Cost-cutting is one of the prime drivers of productivity and this embraces cost reductions at all levels of the organisation. Cost-cutting exercises are not new, and have been a management tool since businesses were formed, but early attempts at cost-cutting were crude. Current cost-cutting exercises, however, are now more sophisticated; they are also becoming universal, as company executives share their knowledge of the options.

Staff cuts – the 80 : 20 method

Perhaps the most traditional form of cost-cutting is increasing the amount of units people have to produce, or the amount of work they have to process, without paying them any more money. By this method you are not reducing the variable costs of the business, you are producing more without incurring extra costs up to the marginal point where other fixed costs may have to be incurred. This traditional productivity-improvement exercise is normally also linked to changes in the work systems in order to facilitate the extra workloads. This method we call the 80 : 20, after Pareto's law. Pareto, an Italian economist in the early years of the century, analysed that in the city where he lived 20% of the population owned 80% of the wealth. This was later picked up by management thinkers who argued that 80% of what we do in business accounts for 20% of the results, and conversely 20% of what we do produces 80% of the results. Efficiency experts now preach that 80% of the combined staff and workforce could easily produce 100% of current activity, thereby indicating that 20% of personnel are surplus to requirements. In the 1970s, and to the mid 1980s, it was very common for companies to embark regularly upon such restructuring programmes. These exercises often led to 20% of employees being 'let go'. By removing work duplications and increasing people's areas of responsibility, it was shown that most organisations were indeed overstaffed. Most companies that went through this process did significantly cut costs in the short run, but employee numbers soon grew again; up to the mid 1980s we observed companies lurching between anorexia and bulimia.

Benchmarking

One of the newer techniques for cost-cutting is benchmarking, which is a method of increasing performance by learning, from other companies, what is the most effective way of doing things. As management began downsizing –

more recently called rightsizing – operations, it became increasingly difficult to calculate the correct number of people needed to run an organisation. Up to a point, executives could downsize staff numbers until the organisation started to squeak, but by then they ran the risk of harming their own business. Management then began to look at other similar companies to compare basic information, and trading results. This is now usually referred to as 'Best in class analysis'.

A company wishing to undertake a benchmarking exercise will need to:

▶ set up a benchmarking team;

▶ identify at least three other companies in the same industry, and producing similar products, that are 'best in class', or at least doing better than you;

▶ obtain as much information about the other companies as possible by analysing their report and accounts, and in some cases visiting them to swap non-sensitive information;

▶ compensate for differences in the organisations as far as possible by recognising, in the necessary calculations, differences in ages of fixed assets, capital structures, etc.

Obviously, most companies will not disclose details of costs, pricing structures, new technology and expansion plans, but their own accounts will indicate turnover, costs of sales, sales per tonne, and other interesting accounting detail. Many companies will be only too pleased to swap notes on Health and Safety and environmental issues, working practices, availability and reliability of some assets and numbers of people engaged in the various activities of the organisation, including long- and short-term contractors. By understanding which are the most efficient businesses in their field, management can take corrective action by identifying the gap between what they are achieving and what is being achieved by their 'best in class' competitors.

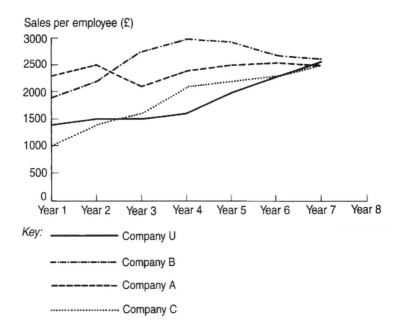

Figure 12.1 '*Best in class' analysis graph*

The graph in Figure 12.1 demonstrates the gap between sales per employee in company U (undertaking the analysis) and three comparable businesses, in seven consecutive years. After compensating for differing assets, management may well decide to cut variable and fixed costs to match the best in class (company A). The 'best in class' figure could also be defined as that of the three most successful competitors, averaged.

Some if the data feeding into this analysis, e.g. numbers of managers to staff, can best be shown graphically to explain how we compare with our competitors. Figure 12.2 shows the staff to management ratio for year 1, the year the benchmark process started. In that year all the competitors had a higher staff : management ratio. Company C, best in class that year, was significantly larger than company U in terms of work-force; company B, however, had the same sized workforce as U and was also achieving higher sales per employee, with a

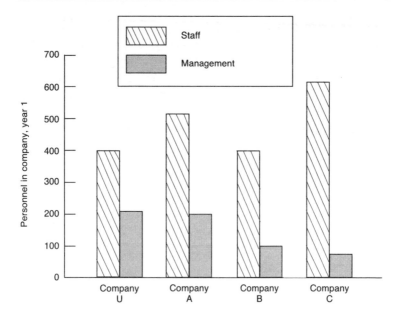

Figure 12.2   *Staff : Management levels*

management half the size. With this type of information, company U's board might well have decided to reduce the numbers of managers and hold the present numbers of staff.

In a major plc that we work for, a 'best in class' analysis clearly showed that their comparative companies were operating with fewer middle managers, and that work could be done as well by more highly trained and developed first-line managers. Through training and development, they had within two years adjusted their ratio of staff to middle managers to the extent that they are now best in class, and being used by their industry as the benchmark. The shift of responsibility from a declining middle management population to first-line managers had the effect of reducing costs and motivating the first-line managers.

Improvement forums

These have been around for a long time, and have been called a variety of names: quality circles, quality work group meetings, best in class meetings, productivity forums, etc. They all had the same prime objective: to reduce costs while at the same time maintaining the high quality necessary for customer satisfaction. Under the general theory that for every pair of hands you get a free brain, it is now recognised that the most effective people to advise management on how to do a job in the most productive manner are those staff actually doing the job. In many ways improvement forums can be regarded as a collective incentive scheme, but in order to maximise their usefulness it is necessary that management offer solid rewards for ideas that produce savings for the organisation. As the National Lottery has proven time and again, people like big prizes and for improvement forums to work to maximum effect the rewards for good ideas must be high.

Re-engineering programmes

A current trend in cost-cutting is to run re-engineering programmes in tandem with benchmarking. Also known as *process engineering*, under these programmes the work systems are observed, recorded and often flow-charted into their component parts, which are then closely scrutinised under the cost-cutting microscope. Improvements are then made to the work-flow systems by various routes – the elimination of unnecessary tasks, unnecessary checking procedures, using machines and technology instead of people. Re-engineering therefore studies the costs of doing a task at the micro level, and through challenging the existing work methods, it enables work patterns to be put back together more efficiently and therefore with less cost. The savings can also be ongoing. Obviously one of the fundamental requirements of work re-engineering is a highly trained and flexible workforce, who are motivated to do the best job with their skill base. (Motivation is a complex subject beyond the scope of this book – but see our book *Managing Your Team*, published by Piatkus.)

Reviewing customer–supplier chains

Significant cost-savings can be found by studying in-depth the costs incurred in the customer–supplier chains. Many companies are continually reviewing their own internal costs, but it is still a relatively new idea to study the costs of getting raw materials to your factory or the costs of sending goods to your customers. This logic applies to internal as well as external customers. It doesn't just mean squeezing a larger discount out of your suppliers, or asking your hauliers to reduce their freight charges; it involves understanding what you are buying and why you are buying it.

This process of study cannot be done in isolation; it is a joint venture between you and your major suppliers and you and your customers, so that cost savings can be shared. This closer working relationship has been described by a senior executive of a retail organisation as 'halving the number of suppliers and distributors and getting into bed with them'. During study of the customer–supplier chain, every aspect of service is considered, i.e. purchasing, warehousing, distribution, transportation, stockholdings, etc., to make sure that the organisations are getting the best value for money.

Outsourcing

Although not very popular with staff in the UK, there has been a general snowballing effect towards outsourcing of activities that are not considered core to the business. Traditional outsourcing has been in the areas of security, canteens, cleaning, and so on, where outside companies provide these services. Because in most of our major organisations staff are fixed costs, outsourcing is usually about reducing such fixed costs to remain competitive.

By outsourcing a function, in the short term you will incur costs of redundancy, outplacement, etc. (Outplacment is a service offering counselling and careers advice, especially to redundant executives, which is paid for by their previous employer.) But in the long run you will save the add-on fixed costs of employing people, because you can reduce indirect fixed costs which are related to the number of people you employ and not to what they do. While no financial director would dispute the considerable savings that have accrued to businesses in outsourcing such functions that can be done just as well (but at less cost) by the outsourcing companies, it is more difficult for management to be as objective when considering outsourcing some other non-core activities, such as accounting and Human Resources.

It is also true that in some companies the reason for outsourcing is not always cost but, rather, lack of expertise in-house, e.g. in Information Technology. In some companies the motivation is to allow management to establish the true cost of running a service, function or department by letting the market determine the rate.

Reducing variable costs

Variable costs vary with production, or the creation of a service. Financial management includes looking to contain and reduce variable costs. The cost of buying in raw materials, partly finished goods, stocks, and utilities should constantly be kept under review by analysing market trends, looking to source from cheaper areas, and understanding where to shop around for cheaper utilities. Consider the latest trend whereby a company based in Manchester can purchase gas, water, and electricity from London, Scotland or Wales, as the now privatised utility companies compete to sell their surplus production. We have all seen notices such as 'Turn off the lights' and 'Is that call really necessary?'; these are indicative of an organisation that wishes to keep its variable costs down. In one large organisation where we work, beside every photocopier there is a notice to the effect that the previous year 400,000 photocopies were made, at a cost of 3.5p each. Such notices are often irritating to staff, but it does keep the issue alive. Variable cost containment, as we are learning from the leaking pipes suffered by some of the water companies, is headline news.

Reducing fixed costs

Fixed costs do not vary with production and therefore have to be paid for irrespective of demand. It is very difficult to reduce fixed costs in the short run because fixed costs are staff costs, depreciation, rent, rates, etc. Staff are often the most valuable asset in a company, and responsible management does not enjoy making staff redundant. Financial managers need to explain fully to colleagues the nature of fixed costs in their sections. In some organisations it is not unusual to find highly paid staff carrying a proportion of fixed cost equal to 50% of their salaries. One of the advantages of reducing manpower is that there is a correlation between fixed costs directly concerned with production and fixed costs concerned with supporting that production. It follows, therefore, that if a number of people are surplus to production requirements then additional cost savings can be achieved by reducing the number of people in the service functions who were there to support them.

EFFECTS UPON PEOPLE

Historically, financial management is normally associated with cost-cutting exercises, and staff often associate cost-cutting with reduction in staff numbers. From our experience, any cost-cutting exercise that is to succeed must be endorsed by all the management and staff. Each department and individual must fully understand why the company is embarking upon such an exercise. To this end, clearly produced graphs and charts are the best medium to explain to staff where the company is, where it wants to get to, and how the company compares with its competitors in a 'best in class' analysis. Staff need to relate cost-cutting with becoming leaders in their field, rather than being threatened with the word 'survival'.

Cost-cutting is a natural and inherent part of a company's development. All companies grow at different rates and

Cost item	Fixed or Variable cost	Balance sheet or Profit & loss	Responsible manager	Annual spend £'000s	Action
Advertising	V	PL	FM	60	Obtain competitive quotes from Splash Advertising Co.
Audit & Accountancy	F	PL	SOL	16	Invite tender from Best Audits & Co.
Bank charges	V	PL	SOL	30	Invite specialist in to run checking IT programme on all accounts
Electricity	V	PL	ARP	38	Obtain quotes from Spark Electricity
Motor lease costs	F	PL	ARP	24	Investigate contract leasing costs
Office rent	F	PL	ARP	52	Negotiate with landlord to purchase office
Rates	F	PL	ARP	8	–
Stationery	V	PL	DG	12	Ask supplier for volume increase discount
Telephone	V	PL	MAK	16	Check what tariffs we are on
Travel	V	PL	DG	26	Reduce by 20%
Depreciation	F	PL	ARP	40	Review annual write-down rates
Stock	F	BS / PL	EH	70	Reduce by 20% within 3 months
Debtors	F	BS	SOL	110	Review 60 days and over: reduce by £30,000 by quarter 2
Creditors	n/a	BS	SOL	14	Pay 45 days instead of present 30 days
Bank overdraft	V	BS	SOL	80	Reduce to £40,000 by quarter 2
Trade investments	n/a	BS	ARP	75	Realise £25,000 to help reduce overdraft

Figure 12.3 *Financial health checklist*

assume responsibilities for services and functions that decline and become obsolete as well as taking on new ones. Information Technology is a good example: larger companies have often tried to do it in-house, only to learn that an expert IT company, able to pool its resources and specialise in that field, can do the job more effectively and at less cost. Persuading staff of the value of cost-cutting is not about selling savings, but about convincing them that it is part of their job to put forward ideas for cost containment and reduction.

FINANCIAL HEALTH CHECK

The financial health checklist in Figure 12.3 is not meant to be exhaustive but an example of how a company might approach cost-cutting exercises with managers responsible for the various items. We recommend that you draw up a financial health checklist for your department and present it to your boss or senior management for consideration. Be prepared to offer recommendations for cost-cutting in your own department.

13

Costing

———◇———

As MORE *and more managers become responsible for running their own departments, they are subject to performance contracts of employment or performance-related reward. If you are in this position, you need to understand costing: how costs are established, how they are grouped for accounting convenience or applied to your department. And every manager concerned with production needs to understand the way production costs are broken down. After reading this chapter, examine the costs applied to your department and be ready to challenge the basis of allocation or apportionment so that you can secure for yourself the best opportunity to improve your position.*

IN AN ever-competitive society, all businesses and organisations, in both the public and private sectors, need to make – and are often required to make – the best possible use of resources at their disposal: personnel, finance and physical assets. Managements of organisations are accountable to the owners in the private sector, and to government or government appointees in the public sector. For this reason, cost-accounting techniques have been developed as a tool to inform the decision-makers how and where money has been spent.

The financial accounts of a business tell you historically what has happened; the management accounts tell you how you are doing and if you are on course as compared with your plan (budget). Cost-accounting is the micro end of the internal accounting function: it examines in as much detail as needed what the money and quantitative inputs and outputs to the business are, so as to establish what it costs to purchase raw materials, produce goods, hold stock, hold a meeting, provide a service, and so on.

A cost can be defined as the amount of money which has been spent or will be incurred in the normal course of business in bringing a product or the supply of a service to its present condition and to its present location. This means that organisations that wish to learn more about their costs than just reviewing the financial and management accounts will put in place cost-recording systems, the aim of which is to give to the responsible line-managers the information necessary to manage and control each part of the business.

The purpose of any costing system should be:

1. To record all the activities undertaken within the organisation so that profitable and unprofitable tasks can be identified, thereby enabling management to take corrective action as needed.

2. To record and analyse all costs incurred so that wastage can be highlighted, and to provide a general framework for ongoing control.

3. To build up a picture of costs so that variances between actual and planned can be seen, and comparisons can also be made with previous months, quarters, years, etc., and with other companies in similar industries.

4. To provide raw data for financial planning and analysis, project costing, estimating and pricing.

Although the objectives of all costing systems in businesses are usually the same, the level of detail required is for management to decide. Striking a balance between level of detail required and the cost of collecting the information will often depend upon the type of business, its size, and the complexity of the work process.

A sole trader of a small business will be able to survive

very successfully without a complicated costing system, carrying around in his/her head sufficient knowledge of the business to enable him/her to estimate and price work and make a profit.

One of the authors received through his letterbox the following flyer:

> *'A room that needs brightening up? Have it completely repainted in a day for £150. This includes two coats of emulsion to the ceiling, two coats of emulsion to the walls. All woodwork rubbed down and filled; one coat of self-undercoating gloss.'*

No sophisticated costing system here, just years of experience on how to do the job.

Small partnerships may also not need a detailed costing system, but if the partners are dealing with one or more customers or clients a week it is sensible to introduce a time sheet so that the partners know whom to invoice, and for what, and to calculate the utilisation of partners and staff.

Larger organisations, of necessity, will need to cost in greater detail so that costing information can be sent down the line. In designing a costing system, accountants cannot work in isolation, although to some it may appear that sometimes they do. They will need to consult at all levels of the business so that they can establish what manpower, materials and overheads are used, where costs can be collected (pooled under a general heading), counted and how, and where convenient cut-off points can be established, in production and process and clerical work systems. Accountants will also need to discuss with line management the level of detail needed.

When building a factory or office, there is very little point in costing items of insignificant value, e.g. paper clips used, which should more properly be collected with other like items under a general heading of stationery. Some organisations, however, cost things so accurately that small cost items are important. If you are spending £90 a night for a hotel room it is irritating to be charged 40p for a newspaper. Obviously in companies of size, where there is more than one outlet, factory, warehouse, etc., it is essential to apply common cost-accounting systems across the whole organisation.

Cost-accounting systems are evolutionary and should be updated and refined in the light of technology and changing management information requirements. They should also take into account available aids to costing, for example:

▶ meters for recording the variable usage of gas, electricity, etc;

▶ installing on-line analysers instead of collecting lab samples;

▶ bar code applications for stock-taking and EPOS (electronic point-of-sale) systems;

▶ time sheets to record staff utilisation;

▶ a weigh-bridge to ascertain amounts on-loaded or off-loaded.

These can remove a great deal of the tedium of traditional methods of analysing and collecting data for costing systems.

COSTING TERMINOLOGY

Let us consider some of the more common terms used in costing. Several of these – fixed costs, variable costs, semi-variable costs, and marginal costs – are examined in chapter 14 on break-even analysis.

Cost unit

A cost unit is a quantity produced (e.g. a motor car) or a service undertaken (e.g. a dental treatment) or a time spent (e.g. an hour with your solicitor), in relation to which the costs of the operation may be conveniently collected.

Cost centre

A cost centre can be a location (such as a factory, office, department) or an item of equipment (e.g. a CAT scanner) or an entity (such as a film production unit) or a person (e.g. a rock star), where costs may be collected and related to cost units.

Cost allocation

Under cost allocation, easily identifiable costs are charged directly to a cost unit or a cost centre. For example, the cost of the gold, for a gold filling, is charged directly to the patient, as is the dentist's time.

Cost apportionment

Where costs cannot be directly allocated to a specific cost unit, it is necessary to apportion them to cost units or cost centres by an agreed formula. For example:

▶ the rent cost may be apportioned to plants on an industrial site in relation to the area of ground they use;

▶ the cost of the Human Resources department may be apportioned to the number of people working in each of the other departments, when calculating the overhead costs of each department;

▶ the costs of running the stores may be apportioned to the value of stores holdings that each department has;

▶ some costs are apportioned by negotiation and agreement among management, for example restructuring costs may be charged to the more profitable divisions of a business, rather than bring others into losses.

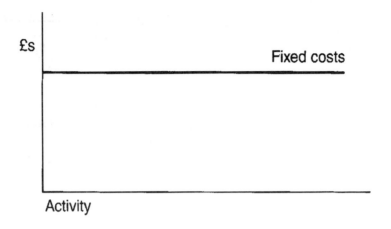

Fixed costs

Fixed costs are those costs that tend to remain unchanged in total for a short term, even if activity increases. Examples of fixed costs are rent, rates, salaries, some insurance costs.

Variable costs

Variable costs are those costs which change directly in relation to changes in activity and volumes. Examples of variable costs are gas, electricity, raw materials.

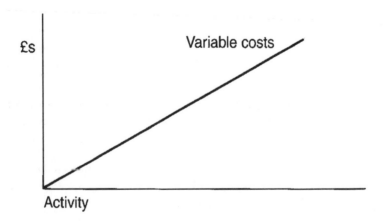

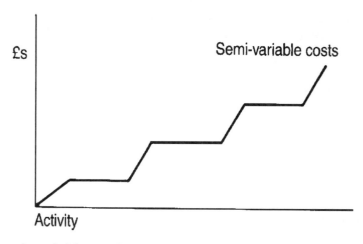

Activity

Semi-variable costs

Semi-variable costs exhibit some of the characteristics of both fixed and variable costs. An example of a semi-variable cost is the wages of extra temporary staff taken on to cope with a short-term increase in workload.

Marginal cost

The marginal cost is the cost of producing one unit of product or service which would not be incurred if that unit were not produced. For example, if all fixed costs are covered by current activity (i.e. sales), then the cost of producing one more sale will be only a variable cost.

Total costing

Total cost is the sum of fixed and variable (or semi-variable) costs. In total costing, the total costs of producing a product or service are charged directly to the product. This is usually only used when a specific product or service is being produced without the necessity of separating the fixed and variable costs. For example, if you make or build something as a one-off, or provide a once-only service, you need only know the total cost so as to establish what to charge the customer. Presumably an accomplished portrait painter, or other artists, takes this costing view when pricing his or her work.

Standard cost

A standard cost is a unit of measurement which is agreed by management. It could be an hourly rate of labour, or a budget period. It is the basis of variance analysis which we will consider in the chapter on budgets and budgeting.

Variable costing

Here the actual recorded costs of producing or doing something are compared to the standard costs, so that management can take necessary action if the variance is negative and significant.

Activity-based costing

This form of costing is becoming increasingly popular. Here, where a specific activity can be identified and where all the costs can be charged, the total cost of the activity can be established. Being a 'people-based' costing system, it does need the use of time sheets. For example, the most important cost for the repair of a gas boiler is usually the attendance and period of work of the repairer. Provided the time sheet is kept accurately and the repairer also records materials used, a clear cost picture can emerge.

Example of costing out a gas boiler repair

As the cost accountant of Gasgo Ltd, you are required to calculate an invoice for A. Punter who recently had a boiler repaired. You are given the following information by R. Ipoff, one of your fitters, on a job sheet:

<table>
<tr><td colspan="2" align="center">**Gasgo Ltd**
Job sheet</td></tr>
<tr><td>Job No.</td><td>*726*</td></tr>
<tr><td>Travelling time</td><td>*1 hr*</td></tr>
<tr><td>Time in attendance</td><td>*2 hrs*</td></tr>
<tr><td>Parts used:</td><td>*One Flood-U-Like pump*
Two fixing brackets</td></tr>
<tr><td>**The system was tested and working**
Fitter's comments</td><td>*System is noisy*</td></tr>
</table>

Obviously, even the most creative accountant cannot accurately cost out this job on the above information, but Gasgo's costing system gives all the necessary additional information:

One standard hour of labour is charged at £55 per hour

Travelling time is charged at £38 per hour

One Flood-U-Like pump is charged at £72

One fixing bracket is charged at £1.20

For explanation, let us consider this costing information and Gasgo's invoice for this job.

One standard hour
The standard hour of labour will include the salary and other costs of employment of the fitter, plus an 'uplift' to cover overheads both fixed and variable, e.g. rent, rates, insurance, depreciation of fitter's tools, management time (fixed) and solder, wire, etc. (variable). The costing system will have calculated these costs using the methods described in the previous pages, and adding on the profit element required by

Gasgo Limited

Invoice No 8742626   Date 8.2.97

To: A Punter
17 Darthill
G74 1LL

Description of work

To repair of boiler, fitting new pump, checking in working order		Fitter: R. Ipoff Job No: 726	
1.	Labour	2 hrs standard	£110.00
2.	New pump		72.00
3.	2 brackets		2.40
4.	Travel	1 hr	38.00
		Total cost VAT @ 17.5%	222.40 38.92
		Invoice total	£261.32

Gasgo. This method of calculation is called *full charge-out rate recovery*. Note that it is not unusual for a person to have two separate charge-out rates, related to two different activities.

Travelling time
The cost of travel will include the fitter's salary and add-on costs, depreciation of the van, running costs such as petrol, servicing, etc., and van insurance.

Pump and fixing brackets
These charges will reflect the cost of the pump and brackets as purchased from the supplier plus an uplift to recover the costs of storing, insurance, etc.

Any costing system will be designed to group costs under convenient general headings, for example:

▶ labour;

▶ materials;

▶ overheads.

These, in turn, can be divided into Direct and Indirect costs (see below).

TOTAL COSTING

From this information you can now build up a picture of how total costs are made up.

Let us assume that your costing system provides you with the breakdown of costs shown below.

Costs summary*	Costs (£)	Consolidation†
Marketing	10,000	To selling costs
Factory labour	16,000	To direct labour costs
Office and accommodation	4,000	To administration costs
Warehouse	8,000	To distribution expenses
Raw materials	50,000	To direct materials costs
Production	11,000	To direct expenses
Factory overheads	3,000	To direct expenses
Administration salaries	5,000	To administration expenses
Distribution	14,000	To distribution expenses
Sales force	22,000	To selling expenses
Depreciation of production assets	6,000	To direct expenses
Factory rent	5,000	To direct expenses
Advertising	10,000	To selling expenses
Total cost	£164,000	

*As collected (grouped) in the Costing/Accounting system.
†The generic headings under which, for simplicity, the costs will be consolidated for ease of presentation to management.

Before drawing up the total cost model let us first define some of the terms used.

Direct costs

Direct costs are those which can be charged to or allocated to cost centres or cost units specifically concerned with *production* of goods or services. Examples are raw materials, labour, production equipment.

Prime cost

The sum of all direct costs – labour (wages), materials, plant and equipment, factory overheads and depreciation of production assets. In effect, at this stage the product is finished and can be handed over to sales and distribution.

Indirect costs

All other costs incurred in supporting the production and

	£'000
Direct labour	16
Direct materials	50
Other direct expenses	25
Prime cost	91
Add:	
Administration	9
Distribution	22
Selling	42
	73
Total cost	164
Mark up 10% (profit)	16
Selling price	£180

Figure 13.1　*Calculation of total cost*

sale of the product – administration, distribution, marketing, sales effort, etc.

We can now build up a total cost model, as shown in Figure 13.1.

It is important to recognise that, although the costing system will indicate the cost it takes to produce or buy an item, it does not mean that you can automatically undertake production and sell the item at a price which makes the process worthwhile. The market dictates the price according to the laws of supply and demand, sometimes taking into account seasonal adjustments. The cost analysis provides a way of determining whether you can economically enter that market, or alternatively the basis for analysing those parts of your activity where your competitors appear to be achieving what you cannot.

14

Break-Even Analysis

◇

A *PICTURE is worth a thousand words – and this applies very much to the presentation of financial information.*

Let us remember Micawber: 'My other piece of advice, Copperfield,' said Mr Micawber, 'you know. Annual income twenty pounds, annual expenditure nineteen and six, result happiness. Annual income twenty pounds, annual expenditure twenty pounds nought and six, result misery. The blossom is blighted, the leaf is withered, the God of day goes down upon the dreary scene, and – and in short you are for ever floored. As I am!'

From *David Copperfield*

BREAK-EVEN ANALYSIS is a very important tool for understanding the relationships between costs and income, and it can be illustrated both numerically and graphically. As chapter 13 on *Costing* explained, if we add fixed costs to variable costs we get a total cost. At the point where income (i.e. sales revenue) is the same as total cost, we reach a break-even situation. If income then exceeds the break-even point, the organisation moves into profit. Break-even analysis enables us to study the effects of increases and decreases in fixed costs, variable costs and income.

To calculate the break-even point of any business, you need to know the fixed costs, the volume of sales, the variable costs per unit, and the selling price per unit of a product or service. Businesses are dynamic – in reality, costs and income are constantly changing – but it is best to consider break-even analysis in a static sense. In order to do this we make the following assumptions:

1 That all costs are either fixed or variable (therefore treat-

ing semi-variable costs as either fixed or variable).

2   That fixed costs remain constant. (Of course, at a given point of increase in activity a business will have to incur additional fixed costs in order to meet the new level of sales. These increases in fixed costs can be people, plant and machinery or even a new factory.)

3   That variable costs vary in direct proportion to activity. (This, of course, is not normally the case, as variable costs do vary out of proportion to activity: suppliers of goods and services offer rebates and discounts depending on the amounts you are buying from them.)

4   That over the activity range under investigation, both costs and revenue behave in a linear fashion.

5   That the only factor affecting costs and revenue is activity (volume).

6   That technology, production methods, and efficiency are constant and unchanging.

7   That the break-even analysis relates only to one product or service or to a constant product and/or service mix.

8   That stock levels remain constant.

To calculate the break-even point, within the limitations of the above assumptions, you can apply the following formula:

$$\text{Break-even point} \ = \ \frac{\text{Fixed costs}}{\substack{\text{Selling price} - \text{Variable costs} \\ \text{per unit} \qquad\quad \text{per unit}}}$$

This can also be explained as follows: sales revenue per unit, less variable costs per unit, equals a £ *contribution* to fixed costs. This is the definition we will use on our ratios to follow. As fixed costs will eventually be recouped by a given number of such contributions, then every sale after the break-even point is a contribution to profit. (At least, up to the point where the business can calculate that more fixed costs will have to be incurred if demand for the goods or services is to be met.) This formula is shown again as 'break-even point by units' (formula 1) below.

BREAK-EVEN FORMULAE

Because of the fourth assumption we have had to make – treating costs and revenue in a linear manner – we can apply certain formulae to calculate break-even points and other related accounting ratios. The following worked examples will help you decide what formula to use in order to discover each piece of information you want.

Known information:
The selling price of a unit is £25, and the variable cost is £20, so the contribution per unit is £5. Fixed costs are £50,000.

1 *Break-even point by units =*

$$\frac{\text{Fixed costs}}{\text{Contribution per unit}}$$

i.e. $\dfrac{£50,000}{5} = 10,000$ units

2 *Break-even point in £s sales =*

$$\frac{\text{Fixed costs x sales price}}{\text{Contribution per unit}}$$

i.e. $\dfrac{£50,000 \times £25}{£5} = £250,000$

3 *The contribution sales ratio =*

$$\frac{\text{Contributon per unit x 100}}{\text{Sales price per unit}}$$

i.e. $\dfrac{£5 \times 100}{£25} = 20\%$

(This, you will recognise, is the gross profit % per unit.)

4 *Level of sales needed to produce a target profit of £20,000, in units =*

$$\frac{\text{Fixed costs + target profit}}{\text{Contribution per unit}}$$

i.e. $\dfrac{£50,000 + £20,000}{£5}$ = 14,000 units

5 *Level of sales needed to produce a target profit of £20,000 in £s sales =*

$$\frac{(\text{Fixed costs + target profit}) \times \text{sales price per unit}}{\text{Contribution per unit}}$$

i.e. $\dfrac{(£50,000 + £20,000) \times £25}{£5}$ = £350,000

Although, as we have said, these calculations are made on the assumption that variable and fixed costs do not change, where such changes are known, the formula can be applied with the updated information. For example, let's assume that you have established that fixed costs are going to rise by £10,000 per annum, and that variable costs are expected to increase by £1 per unit. However, because of the market conditions, you don't want to raise the selling price per unit. You can calculate the volume of sales needed to maintain a profit of £20,000 by applying formula 4 above. Firstly you must recalculate the contribution per unit: £25 (selling price, as before) minus £21 (new variable cost) = £4.

Applying formula 4 gives us the following calculation:

$$\frac{£60,000 + £20,000}{£4} = 20,000 \text{ units}$$

Accordingly, you will have to sell a further 6,000 units to achieve your target profit of £20,000.

As previously mentioned, the break-even point can be drawn graphically. Formulae 1 and 2 can both be shown as in Figure 14.1. In our experience, management often prefer financial information in this form, so long as they have detailed information to back up the graphs.

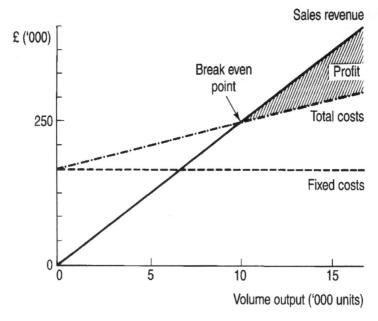

Figure 14.1   *Break-even point*

The diagram shows break-even is at £250,000, or 10,000 units where sales revenue equals total costs.

Let's now examine the uses of break-even analysis as a management and financial tool.

USES OF BREAK-EVEN ANALYSIS

Selling price analysis

The effects of increases or decreases in the selling price per unit can be calculated and represented to management graphically. This can be of particular use for monitoring the effects of discounts, rebates, etc., as well as establishing the necessary selling prices to maintain target profits as influenced by changes to fixed and variable costs.

Sales targets

It follows that if the market will not stand an increase in the selling price, then the additional sales needed to maintain target profits can be calculated. This is, of course, useful in discussing and setting sales targets with sales forces and agents.

Changes in variable costs and use of fixed assets

Increases and decreases in fixed and/or variable costs, once calculated, can be predicted and the calculation will show the effect on the profitability of the business. Analysis can be used to show the impact of better buying practices, cost-reduction programmes, and more efficient use of fixed assets, etc.

'Make or buy' decisions

If demand for a company's goods or services increases, then the variable costs will increase in direct proportion to the increase in activity. (Although, as mentioned before, unit-variable costs can increase and/or decrease in a non-linear fashion with such changes in activity.) However, there will come a point when management will have to take a decision whether or not to increase fixed costs to meet demand. This could be the purchase of additional fixed assets, e.g. plant and machinery, or indeed taking on more staff. If increased demand is expected to be maintained, management may well decide to invest in additional fixed costs. If, however, the increase in demand is thought to be a temporary blip then management may well decide, if possible, to meet the increase in demand by buying in finished or partially finished goods as an alternative to incurring extra fixed costs. In this case break-even analysis is a useful tool to help management make the most cost-effective decision.

Special orders

Once a firm, or a product or service, has broken even and therefore moves into profit, management has a great deal more manoeuvrability in making financial decisions. For instance, if a firm is offered a special order by a new or existing customer but at a sales price below the norm, as long as the firm has broken even, the sales order can be accepted if variable costs are covered; each sale or unit from the special order will make a further contribution to profit even though that contribution is lower than that for the company's other sales. The benefit continues up to the point where additional fixed costs have to be incurred. (Normally special orders, contracts, etc., are one-off as no management will want to risk offending present customers by consistently offering lower prices to other parties.)

Sales mixes

Sales mixes are an interesting area for consideration. It is very unusual for companies to produce only one product or service in the long run. Often companies need to produce different products, not only to supply customer needs but also to maximise use of fixed assets. One way to make best use of assets is to investigate what other products could sensibly be produced with the same assets. Some chemical companies have, for some years now, been constructing dual-capacity plants as a hedge against slackening demand for a product. The classic business case study for this is Walls' sausages and ice cream. In the days before deep refrigeration and household freezers were common, Walls increased the use of their assets, and thereby increased contribution to fixed costs, by producing sausages in the autumn and winter when demand was at its highest, and ice cream in the spring and summer, using the same machinery and staff. (But hopefully not the same raw materials!) By this means, both sausages and ice cream broke even at a much lower level of sales than if each had incurred separate fixed costs.

Keeping marginal plants in operation

Sooner or later, firms that don't make a profit will go out of business, as their sources of finance dry up because they can't service a return on the investment for the owners and/or pay interest on a loan. However, in a multi-plant business producing a range of products, where, say, three out of four are profitable, then break-even analysis can help in assessing the effects of the loss. If the plant which is loss-making is unable to cover its variable costs in the medium-to-long run, management will normally close it. However, if the plant is covering its variable costs and making a contribution to the fixed costs of the organisation, then in our experience, a sensible management will continue running the plant in the short term and, through a cost-cutting exercise, try to make the plant more profitable. If the unprofitable plant were to close, and fixed costs relating to that plant could not be totally eradicated, the remaining three profitable plants would have to pick up the residual fixed costs, which would not make financial sense. This explains why unprofitable situations are often continued in the short run.

Mothballing

One of the older examples of financial decision-making was the Cornish tin mines. The mines were maintained so that when the price of tin rose, they could be opened and when the price fell, they could be closed. If the price rose steeply then new mines were dug.

In business, some plants and/or factories become unprofitable as demand (and therefore prices) for their products fall. Unlike, say, in the retail trade where closing a branch shop can be a relatively simple process, closing down a plant is much more complex. At what point do we close, and then scrap it? As explained above, it may be sensible to keep an unprofitable plant open as long as it is covering its variable costs and making some significant contribution to fixed costs. 'Mothballing' a plant is an alternative to scrapping it –

it can be re-opened when the price of the product has increased and/or the variable costs (e.g. costs of materials) have decreased. Again, break-even analysis can plot the significant trends.

Outsourcing decisions

In properly organised and well conducted businesses, permanent staff are now always regarded as a fixed cost. It follows, therefore, that in any fixed-cost reduction programmes, staff are often made redundant. To hedge against this (which can be costly for the organisation), companies now increasingly outsource some services to contracting companies (see page 122). The financial benefit in the short run is moving staff costs from fixed costs to variable costs, because contracted staff can be 'turned on' or 'turned off' to meet changing needs. A break-even chart will demonstrate the effect of using contractors, showing how far fixed costs will be reduced.

Investment decisions

In some circumstances, a product and/or service can be produced or supplied in various ways, using plant, equipment, technology and manpower in different amounts. Each of these requires investment, and break-even analysis can assist management in deciding which investment route looks more attractive.

For example, motor cars can be robot-manufactured, creating high fixed costs due to the high level of investment in technology, or they can be manufactured manually with lower (fixed) costs from technology investment and higher manpower costs. (Note that, in many countries where cars are made, manpower is a variable cost.) The same applies to agriculture, where you can run the organisation with a high fixed cost (machinery) and low variable cost (farm labour), or low fixed costs and high variable costs.

Some economists argue that one of the differences between

the UK manufacturing industry and the German model is that in the UK we have traditionally elected for low fixed-cost plant and factories (therefore using higher variable costs), whereas the Germans have invested heavily in plant and other assets, so successfully that they are also able to employ people at higher wages than in the UK.

15

Budgets

———◇———

A FEW YEARS AGO a bank manager, a friend of one of the authors, decided with his wife to quit the 'rat race' in London and move, with their children, to the Lake District. There they purchased a general store, with off-licence and a sub post office. Some time later, in reply to a letter asking how they were getting on, they replied, 'Overdraft down, stock up, so we must be doing OK.'

Sole traders can take a comparatively relaxed approach to the budgetary process. Small businesses certainly don't need the complex budgetary control systems outlined in this chapter, but every successful business does need some degree of financial control through budgeting. As a manager, you should insist on your involvement in the budget process. Any company which seeks to maximise its potential from its budgeting will respect your requests to be involved and take responsibilities, and will try to meet your need for feedback.

CHAPTER 13 on *Costing* showed that larger companies need to evaluate in detail what it costs to produce goods or services, so that comparison and control can be exercised by management. Budgeting, or setting a budget, is the process of setting financial and quantitative standards and targets for an organisation's activities and agreeing them with individual budget holders, so that the necessary resources can be allocated. Budget standards are written either in quantities (e.g. the number of hours needed to complete a job) or in financial language (e.g. the hourly rate in £/p), or in both (e.g. 60 hours at £10 an hour). A budget holder's target might be to achieve a certain quarterly income, working to these standards. So budget holders need to agree both the standards and the targets to which they have to work, and both must be meaningful, achievable and flexible to take into account the organisation's evolving circumstances.

A budget is a bit like a road map: it sets out what direction we are going in, what route we are taking, and how many miles we must travel to get to our destination; we can also see when, and how far, we are off course. Most people are conversant with the concept of budgeting from running their own personal finances; to our minds, a budget – whether personal or in business – should not be regarded as a restraining control system, stopping us from spending money, but as permission to spend money on resources in order to achieve a pre-arranged set of objectives. Budgeting and budgetary control are important management tools to help managers plan and agree targets, and then compare, weekly, monthly, quarterly and annually, what was planned to happen against what actually did happen. Any differences to the plan, positive or negative, are called *variances*. Variances can be reviewed at any time and necessary action can then be taken.

Variances, just like standards, can be either in quantity or in money, or in both. Take our example of a budget for a job of £600, made up of an expected 60 hours' work at £10 an hour. The actual cost turns out to be £640. You need to know if the number of hours was at variance, or the £ amount per hour. It might be that the end result came from 64 hours at the agreed rate of £10, or the agreed 60 hours at a rate of £10.66 an hour; equally, it might be the result of 40 hours at £16 per hour or 80 hours at £8 per hour. You can't take corrective action until you know what went wrong. Budgetary control is the monitoring of how actual activity compares with budgeted activity, and the action taken on the results.

SETTING THE BUDGET

The budget process, in general terms, follows the pattern shown in Figure 15.1.

The input to the budget committee, who are charged with developing the budget, comes from various sources:

Past results and past performance

The company's accounting department, in particular, will assist in collecting and comparing the data of past actual results and past actual performances as a guideline to what might be expected to happen in the future. At the same time, they will also examine the variances of various departments: they will look at the budgets as submitted by, and negotiated by, departments previously and compare them to the actual results to see which departments appear to be realistic, and which have come in over or under-budget. This will enable the budget committee to place more or less reliance on the current budget forecasts from those departments.

Organisational objectives and long-range plans

The budget is a way of measuring the progress towards the achievement of the company's overall objectives and perceived mission. Someone should be involved in the budget committee to oversee that this is the case. We are familiar with several companies where very effective budgets have been prepared and, separately, very laudable mission statements have been created, but where the two are almost at odds with each other. The inevitable result of such a disjointed policy is that the company is being driven down two roads at the same time. In such cases, variance analysis of actual performance against budgeted performance often engenders a hostile debate with the company's management dividing into two factions, each arguing their side and both believing that they are complying with the framework they

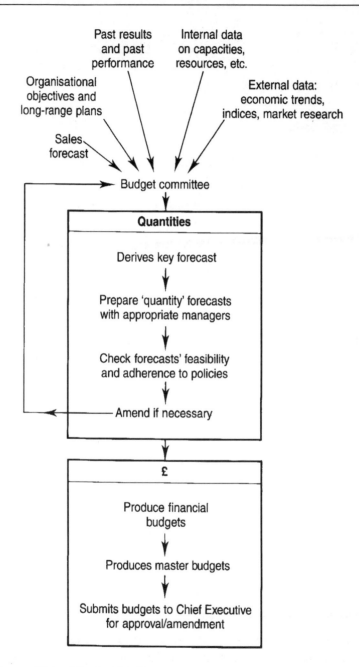

Figure 15.1 *The budgeting process*

have been given. And, of course, they are: some are following the organisation's stated objectives and some are following the budget plans. So the two must merge at the earliest possible point.

Initial data

Internal data on capacities, resources, etc.

All departments will be asked to report their perceived resources, e.g. skillforce, workforce, material, technology. They will be asked to predict their capacity using these resources to best effect. This data gives the budget committee some idea of what total resources are presently available.

External data: economic trends, indices, market research

The budget committee will take into account changing technology, changing market demands, opinions, the activities of competitors, and so on.

Sales

In many companies, the main influence on their budgets is, initially, their sales forecast. The budget committee receives information on unfulfilled orders already placed at the time the budget process gets underway. In some companies this can be several hundred million pounds' worth of orders, particularly where many projects are long-term. In addition to this, the sales force and marketing departments will be asked to predict further sales likely to arise during the period of the budget.

The budget committee

The budget committee will be composed of representatives from all the main activities of the company – production, sales, marketing, and so on – and coordinated by members of the finance department. They will often start from the sales forecast, ensure that this is accurate given the external data, confirm that the forecasts meet the organisational objectives and long-range plans and, most important, they will ensure that if increased sales are expected, they can be met by existing capacities and resources. Where there is imbalance between an increased sales forecast and the resources needed to meet it – and there usually is in the initial stages of budget preparation – then the first focus of the budget committee will be to discover the extent to which existing resources can be stretched, realigned or expediently expanded to accommodate the increase in sales. At some point here, a contingency will be put into place: if the company commits itself to try to meet sales which it doesn't currently have the resources to meet, it will account for the possibility that not all sales will come through; but it will also provide for the possibility that orders will come through by budgeting for increasing resources in the short term, e.g. agreeing overtime rates, identifying sources of new staff, costing and planning for additional production, outsourcing, warehousing, and so on.

Derives key forecast

The budget committee, having deliberated all of the above, will produce a forecast of what it believes the company is capable of achieving in the year ahead.

Prepares quantity budgets with appropriate managers

Having identified the end of the journey, i.e. the total expected sales and resultant activity for the year ahead (or period of the budget) the budget committee then 'tracks back', breaking down the activity into quantities for the appropriate departments. It does so with the cooperation of, and additional input of, the appropriate departmental managers, who are therefore 'buying into' the budget at an early stage. This gives budgetary control a higher chance, as the managers are committed to the budget's success and don't feel that it has been imposed on them. The committee then drafts these quantity budgets.

Checks feasibility and adherence to policies of quantity budgets

Each manager will be asked to report back on their perception of the likelihood that the departmental budget is accurate and that it complies with what they believe their department's role is within the company.

Amends if necessary

From this point, there is a continual loop-back in the process, up to the budget committee and down again, where gradually a refinement takes place based on the input of the managers and the (often contradictory) wishes of senior management.

Produces financial budgets

Once the quantity budgets have been agreed, then the accountancy department will translate these into financial budgets equating sales and resources to £s in and £s out, and thus to expected profits and cashflows. (See the cashflow forecast in chapter 7. This is a form of budget, broken down into months.)

Produces master budgets

Once financial budgets have been produced for each department, these are amalgamated into a master finance budget which is again checked to the overall master plan for the company for the budget period.

Submits budgets to chief executive for approval/amendment

For the budget to succeed, there must be the approval and support of senior management. This is the point at which the budget becomes policy. Senior management should make their support for the budget as visible as possible in order that those with the task of implementing it 'at the coal face' know that their successes will gain the approval of their bosses and their failures will also gain their attention. Both of these are motivational in their own way.

Why budget?

The objectives of any budgeting system are as follows:

▶ to set the goals and objectives of the business and to write them in quantitative, qualitative and financial terms so that management and budget holders are clearly aware of their responsibilities, accountabilities and limits of authority.

▶ to calculate, and draw up, an agreed set of standards by which each division, department, and section agrees to be measured.

▶ to agree the process that will measure efficiency and effectiveness of the company by highlighting the extent to which objectives are being met within the resources of the organisation.

▶ to show variances, which will be the basis for deciding what action to take when the business is seen to be off course.

The question now arises as to who constructs the budget and how. As is often the case in financial management, there are no hard and fast rules, and the budgetary process is always dependent upon the size and complexity of the organisation. Problems further arise in trying to set a budget for a completely new product or service, e.g. the Channel Tunnel. Although many of the tasks required in building the tunnel had been done before, and standards were no doubt set, the tunnel budget was grossly overspent. Budgets are a combination of historical data, experience, and clever estimating. Obviously, the more a process, or a fabrication, or a business, is budgeted the more accurate it gets; no doubt the proposed building of a tunnel under the straits of Gibraltar will take into account the lessons learned from the building of the Channel Tunnel.

Remember that there is only one master budget. All smaller budgets within the organisation are only part of the master budget, which is in essence a financial model of the organisation.

There is no limit to the number of budgets an organisation may draw up, but usually budgets are drawn up by function and/or organisational requirements. An example of the components of a master budget is shown opposite.

This example relates to a manufacturing and trading organisation, and is not meant to be an exhaustive list. You can see how the breakdown is similar to the one on page 137 in chapter 13 on *Costing*.

Obviously, the budgets shown may also be broken down further into sectional budgets. For example, the advertising budget may be split into budgets for radio, television and press advertising; the transport may be split into road, rail and sea transport. The number of budgets to be formulated will be for controlling managers to decide, in conjunction with the professional accountancy staff. The decision will be based on what is needed for the sensible control and coordination of the business.

You will notice that the above budgets relate to the profit and loss account of the business. Some budgets, however, relate to the balance sheet of the organisation so that some companies will draw up a budget for:

▶ stock

▶ cash

▶ capital expenditure.

The master budget

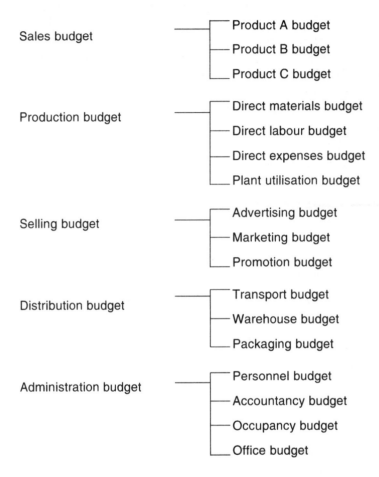

Normally, the design of the organisation chart will determine under what headings the budgets will fall; for instance, in the example of the master budget we have shown, the sales budget will be under the control of the sales director; the production budget will be under the control of the production director; the selling budget will be under the control of the marketing and operations director; and so on.

Let's examine two components of a master budget in more detail.

Sales budget

All sales directors tell us that it is very difficult to project a sales budget accurately unless you are a monopoly. This is probably true, but all companies still have to estimate what number of products or services will be sold. The person responsible for the sales budget will be the sales director, who in turn will consult with the area managers and, both directly and indirectly, with the sales teams.

It's not enough to take last year's budget, add on a factor for inflation, and then pray! Professional budgeting needs to take into account some or all of the following information:

▶ the sales objectives of the organisation, including possibilities for growth, new markets and areas, and new product introduction;

▶ financial analysis of past performance, split into product groups and/or sales representatives and/or customers;

▶ current information regarding the ability of the organisation to fulfil its objectives;

▶ external information: environmental issues, cyclical trading patterns, market research, etc.

Cash budget

One of the more important budgets is the cash budget, drawn up by the financial controller or chief accountant. A company's ability to survive in the short run is its ability to have sufficient cash resources to meet all its liabilities, including servicing debt interest and loan repayments. The cash budget will reflect the 'sales-to-debtor-to-cash conversion' ratios and, having planned that income, will then plot against it the cash requirements of the organisation, such as payments to suppliers, salaries, overheads, interest etc. Shortfall of funds may have to be financed by overdraft or other borrowings; surplus funds will need investing so that the money is working for the company. The cash budget is therefore an action plan for management which warns when there are periods of shortfalls or surpluses of funds, which will enable management to take corrective action with any number of the financial tools available.

BUDGETARY SYSTEMS

Let us now consider the various types of budgets we can adopt for a business, namely:

▶ a fixed budget

▶ a flexible budget

▶ a zero-based budget

▶ a rolling budget

Fixed budget

As the name suggests, a fixed budget is for a fixed period, and for a fixed amount of income and expenditure. Normally given for a year at a time, the fixed budget sets out the permissible total expenditure by month, quarter, or whatever, which is then compared in detail to the actual expenditure. Monthly variances and cumulative variances are listed. A somewhat rigid system, it normally doesn't take into account changes in activity or other factors affecting the financial results.

Flexible budget

This approach recognises the relationship between activity, fixed costs and variable costs. Accordingly, the budget (or certain items within the budget) are increased or decreased to take into account the increase or decrease in activity. For example, if sales increase by 10% then the knock-on effect on distribution – transport, warehousing and packaging – is calculated pro-rata – or to an agreed formula – and these departmental budgets are increased to finance the extra workload.

Zero-based budget

These are often used in times of financial crisis or after a company has been taken over or merged with another company. The existing budgets are suspended and all budget holders are asked to question and justify any expenditure not directly related to the core activities of the business. The idea is to reduce expenditure for the master budget so that senior management can establish the minimum requirements to run the business. This system deliberately ignores the history which may contain many false assumptions, and starts 'from fresh'.

Rolling budget

This is not exactly a budgetary system. The rolling budget is more a method of updating the budget on a continuous basis. Here the budget, say for a year, is considered as dynamic and each quarter or month the budget is projected for a further twelve- to eighteen-month period, or whatever management deem sensible. If a budget is split into quarters, then as quarter one is finished for year one, quarter one is calculated for year two. The main advantage of rolling budgets is that they get away from the fixed budget mentality and mean that controlling managers do not take their eyes off the ball.

OWNERSHIP OF BUDGETS

For budgets to work effectively, it is essential that certain features are in place, and that the budget process allows for 'ownership', and therefore commitment, by the budget holders.

It should be stressed that budgeting is not an accounting

function. In some companies where accountants are in the driving seat, they prepare budgets and, often with the approval of the board, impose them on the organisation. However, except where the accountant is directly responsible for a section of the organisation (the finance department) he or she is generally the least able to prepare sensible departmental budgets. Accountants are good co-ordinators of budgets and assist by collecting and interpreting information about past performance and converting current expectation into financial terms. But, for budgets to work, they must be a function of the whole management team; each manager must have input to the preparation of their 'local' budget and be involved in negotiations on the coordination of all local budgets into the master budget.

Essential features of budgetary control

1 *Establishment of clear objectives*

Those with the responsibility and authority of implementing the budget – budget holders at all levels – need to be clear as to what it is they are being asked to achieve. You need to know both your range and your limits of authority and responsibilities. Without this you cannot share the effective budget process with your staff.

2 *Senior management support*

Keeping within budget must not be perceived as a function of lower-level management while senior management is neither interested in, nor committed to, the budget. If this is the general perception, those implementing the budgets will believe that the outcomes will have no effect on their careers or short-term rewards such as salary increases. The support of senior management must be present and made highly visible – in some companies there is support but this is not communicated to lower-level management, with the result that the support is worthless.

3 *A realistic preparation timetable*

The budget is essentially a management tool and must be used while the contents are still valid. Information must therefore be gathered together quickly: a 'realistic' preparation timetable in effect means a 'quick' preparation timetable and some accuracy can be sacrificed for speed. The budget committee should communicate that timetable in detail to all those responsible for input to the budget process and stress the deadlines for each stage. Failure to meet the deadlines will result in the budget being out of date, ineffective and irrelevant.

4 *Discussion of submitted budgets*

Throughout the process of budget preparation, managers should have the opportunity to discuss the figures they put forward, and any covering explanations, so that they are motivated to achieve (or exceed) their predictions.

5 *Responsibility for control and achievement*

Once budget centres are established and the responsible manager is identified, senior management should give that manager maximum empowerment to affect activity in that area. The reality is often that although a manager may be in charge of, say, a budget of £1 million, there is flexibility of only a few percent of the total figure because of committed costs – salaries, capital expenditure, and certain allocated costs such as rent, light, heat, and so on. Nonetheless, senior management should communicate this openly, allowing the maximum flexibility realistically available and ensuring that the manager can implement choices as widely as possible to affect the outcome. The finance department should offer appropriate and adequate support to non-financial managers.

6 *Continuous use of approved budgets*

As pointed out at the start of this chapter, the budget is a part of the planning process and must be constantly seen to be part of the way in which management turns its plans, financial and otherwise, into reality. Constant fire-fighting in crisis situations demonstrates either that unrealistic budgets were drawn up, or that they are being ignored (usually both!).

7 *Continuous scrutiny of results against budget*

Budget holders should continuously monitor activity against budget – in other words, exercise budgeting control. As soon as you spot a variance, you need to discover the reason; secondly, in the case of adverse variances, you need to find out if some management control can be implemented to bring activity back into the anticipated line or whether the budget was for some reason inaccurate. If so, you will need a more accurate budget, realistic enough to be motivational again. To be motivational, budgets must be achievable and if they are not adjusted periodically they become increasingly unrealistic and unachievable, and therefore unmotivational. Remember always that a budget is not a straitjacket but a plan within which budget holders operate for as long as circumstances remain unchanged.

16

Financial Analysis and Planning

———◇———

THE AVERAGE line manager's approach to forecasting is often to take last year's figures and increase by some factor, usually the inflation rate. This is simplistic and takes no account of changing markets, costs of money, competition from within the company for use of resources, and so on. Information technology can provide you with a great deal more information on which to make decisions. This chapter sets out the basic, and easiest, tools which allow predictions about the future to be calculated with reference to the current economic and market climate.

FINANCIAL analysis and planning has become a very specialised field within financial management. The combined existence, in some companies, of the 'rocket scientists' (PhDs in mathematics) and sophisticated software means that some of the advanced mathematical tools used are understood by very few people. In this chapter we will avoid space travel and consider some of the more down-to-earth techniques.

FORECASTING

Forecasting is a planning tool to be used before the preparation of the budget. Forecasting is concerned with the *probability* of something happening in response to a given set of circumstances. For instance, if a company halves the price of one of its very popular product lines, we can predict that sales will probably increase. Forecasting in a very fast-changing world, however, is a challenging task and more and more managers are having to turn to new ideas and tools for assistance: the modern financial manager needs more than the skills of Mystic Meg – although there is an element in forecasting beyond 'reading the market right' and entrepreneurial flair, an element which people would just call 'guesswork'.

Probability theory

One technique in forecasting is the use of probability theory. Here the likelihood of an event happening is calculated and recalculated as actual events occur. Probability is used to forecast sales, effects of price increase and price reductions. Lessons learned by the application of probabilities to the business system are recorded and stored in the database for future reference. The technique takes into account two types of behaviour: deterministic and probabilistic. Deterministic behaviour takes into account that an event can be accurately determined from past experience, e.g. we switch on a television set because past experience tells us what will happen as a result. Probabilistic behaviour is action dependent on a result within a wide range of probabilities, e.g. playing a roulette wheel. (So although the probability of winning the National Lottery is around 14 million to 1, deterministic behaviour means that the larger the jackpot, the more people will play. Despite the fact that the odds of certain numbers coming up do not change, more people are inclined to buy a ticket.)

An example of probability theory applied to retailing is the effects of 'stock-outs'. When a company has 'stocked out' (sold out), it needs to record, for future reference, what effect that has upon a customer. If customer A goes into a retail outlet to buy a product and finds it is not available, will the customer walk away from the shop without buying anything, or will he or she purchase a similar (or indeed completely different) product? This is known as the *substitution effect*, and if the retail store can identify the original purchase intention and record the actual purchase then the probable success or failure of this substitution effect can be monitored. This of course assists management in calculating minimum and maximum stock levels.

An interesting branch of probability is Queuing Theory. In those business situations where queue length is critical to customer satisfaction, for example check-out queues in a supermarket and queues at a petrol station, the average lengths of queues can be calculated mathematically using simultaneous equations; action can then be taken to avoid customers rejecting the outlet because of queue length.

Econometric modelling

This is another forecasting technique available to management. It is achieved through the construction of mathematically based models, using computers. The model is constructed from economic data, which are given mathematical values, and the combined effects of these values upon each other, their interdependencies, are computed through a set of equations. Econometric modelling data include such factors as inflation, interest rates, population mixes (e.g. percentages of young people to older people), employment patterns, political stability, lifestyle changes, environmental issues, and many more. The macro model of the UK economy – known as the Treasury Model – is used by the government to forecast the effects of inflation, taxation and interest rates upon 'UK Plc'. Interestingly, we learn from the financial press that independent econometric forecasting models are traditionally more accurate than the Treasury Model.

Probability theory and econometric modelling are just two of the tools used by government and businesses to determine the effects of changes upon the basic financial models (see below). These techniques will then be used to develop sales trends, etc., which are often the fuel that drives most business decisions. Forecasts of sales are, of course, necessary to determine the scale of activity, i.e. production needed to fulfil expected sales.

FINANCIAL MODELLING

A financial model is not a business plan. A business plan is concerned with the owner's goals, objectives, targets, etc., as well as detailed plans for the growth of the company and what resources will be necessary. A financial model is simpler. It is a picture of a business reduced to actual results, expected results, and percentages for ease of understanding. Every company will have some form of financial model, however crude. Even sole traders know the backlog of orders and forward workloads, who owes money, what money is owed and what the state of the bank account is. By reducing the business to mathematical relationships, the effect of a change in one critical area can be input to the model, so that the knock-on effects can be computed. In many ways a financial model is like a flexible master budget (see page 159) that enables management to play 'What If' games with the figures to assist in making decisions.

In the financial model shown in Figure 16.1, let's assume that you have actual figures for year 1 and that management wish to 'play' with the model and look at various projected effects for years 2 to 5 inclusive. By inputting, say, sales projections for years 2 to 5, you can observe the effect that the sales activity will have upon trading profit, net profit, stocks, debtors, cash, and so on. The financial model is therefore a 'macro' look at the whole organisation in financial terms so that 'micro' effects can, in turn, be studied. For example, the model may show that with sales increasing to a certain figure in year 4, the warehouse will not be able to accommodate the increase in stock. You can then use this projected information to plan for an extension to the warehouse. Most of the large companies in the UK have very sophisticated financial models of the organisation and its

	Year 1		Year 2		Year 3		Year 4		Year 5	
	£	%	£	%	£	%	£	%	£	%
Income & Distribution										
Sales										
Overheads										
Trading profit										
Interest paid										
Net profit										
Tax paid										
Dividend paid										
Retained profit										
Assets & working capital										
Stocks										
Debtors										
Cash										
Creditors										
Working capital										
Fixed assets										
Total assets										
Cashflow										
Net cash inflows										
Net cash outflows										
Cash movement (+ or −)										
Financing										
Share capital (+ or −)										
Loans taken out										
Loans repaid										
Finance movements										
Ratio analysis										
Gross profit percentage										
Net profit percentage										
Return on sales										
Sales per employee										
Liquid ratio										
Debtors collection										
Creditors collection										
Stock turn										
ROACE										
Gearing										

Figure 16.1   *Financial model: proforma*

divisions. The larger oil companies play 'What If' with varying oil prices per barrel, so that they can determine what to do at various platforms of prices. Obviously, the corporate financial model is an essential tool for constructing master budgets.

Because the computer model has constant relationships built into it, a change in any proposed figures will automatically show what the effects would be on other assumed figures. You can then play 'What If' games, such as 'If sales were to double, what would be the result on certain costs? on working capital?' and so on. **Use this proforma to play modelling games in your own company.**

The increasing move towards greater disclosure regarding financial information, combined with the fact that quoted companies are always explaining their strategy and tactical plans to financial analysts, means that information about companies is readily available and it is easier for other people to build financial models about companies. The financial analysts produce mirror copies of financial models in order to project share prices in the event of something beneficial or adverse happening. This means that companies themselves have to keep their financial models up to date, test their validity, and – using the information generated – advise senior executives. Many senior resignations from boards of directors result from the analysis of the company's financial model, although those outside don't learn of this until much later. Interestingly, when finance directors resign suddenly, the share price of that company will often go down until it becomes clear on what issue the resignation was based.

INVESTMENT DECISIONS

Payback analysis

These days, because cashflow is such an important factor, most companies look towards the cash generation of an investment decision as the most important limiting criterion in deciding whether or not to proceed.

If a large supermarket chain decides to build a new out-of-town superstore, one of the most important criteria for the financial decision will be the payback period, i.e. how quickly the superstore can be built and 'up and running', so that the checkout tills can start taking cash. Often, the quicker the cash is expected to start being generated, the more likely it is that the investment will be sanctioned.

Payback analysis is also applied to the risk of an investment. If a company, for economic or market reasons, decides that it wants to build an installation in a politically unstable region or country, then the initial investment decision often only makes sense if the company can recover its cash investment in as quick a time as possible, i.e. taking a calculated risk on the likelihood of political and/or economic upheaval.

We will consider payback analysis in more detail in chapter 22, including an example of a capital project and the various criteria which need to be used. Payback analysis is basically concerned with cash inflows over time. It does not indicate the profitability of an investment, nor does it take into account the cost of tying up capital for the length of the investment. Some companies, as part of their financial discipline, set an initial payback period for any investments of, say, eighteen months. This means that they will not sanction projects that do not show a cash inflow within eighteen months.

Discounted cashflow (DCF)

In times of high inflation, most people are aware that the pound in their hand today is worth more than the pound in a year's time. Even leaving aside the factor of inflation, we know that the pound in the hand today can be invested at a given rate of interest in the financial marketplace. Discounted cashflow is very similar to interest being earned in a bank or building society, except that instead of adding the interest on you are discounting it, i.e. taking it off. Calculating DCF is done by a set of tables which give the

| | Value of £100 at inflation rates of: | |
	5%	7.5%
At end of:	£	£
year 1	95	93
year 2	90	87
year 3	86	80
year 4	82	75
year 5	78	69
year 6	74	65
year 7	71	60
year 8	68	56
year 9	64	52
year 10	61	49

Figure 16.2   *Discounted cashflow*

discounted value of money over time at variable rates. For example, let's assume that you have £100 and you decide to put it under the proverbial mattress rather than investing it at the building society at a rate of interest of 5% or a merchant bank at a rate of 7.5%. The decline in the value of the £100 will be as shown in Figure 16.2. For example, at 5%, after seven years your £100 would be worth only £71.

Two main issues stand out from this table, namely that money becomes less valuable over time and that money loses value faster the higher the discount rate. DCF is therefore a tool to show you what you are foregoing if you don't invest and to indicate the cost of investing in alternative projects. DCF is used in calculating the net present value of an investment (see below).

Net present value (NPV)

NPV is another method of assessing the viability of an investment and considering the merits of competing investments. NPV brings together payback analysis and discounted cashflow. Everything has a price and NPV is a financial management tool that is concerned with the cost of capital as well as how quickly the company is going to get its money back. At its simplest, NPV forecasts how much money the investment will earn and then calculates how much that money would be worth in today's terms.

Net present value is calculated as follows. Let's assume you are considering investing in an asset.

1 Establish the discount rate applicable to your company. This can be the return of money you can get by investing it in the financial market; or the return you get from within your own company, i.e. the return of average capital employed (ROACE) (see page 89); or the cost to the company of borrowing money, which will be a mixture of bank and other loan interest average costs and the dividend costs of equity shares.

2 Using forecasting techniques, market research, historical financial data for extrapolation, etc. calculate the expected sales income generated by the proposed investment, i.e. cashflow inwards over the period to be considered, normally the expected life of the asset.

3 Apply the DCF technique to the expected sales income, using the agreed discount rate arrived at in stage 1. Add together all the now-discounted cash inflows, which will give you the net present value of the income from the investment.

4 The result in stage 3 can now be subtracted from the total amounts of funds to be invested. If the inflow of funds (discounted) exceeds the outflow of funds within the payback period set by the company, say two years, then the investment proposal looks a sound proposition.

The profitability of such investment proposals are measured by the return on the investment (ROI) and return on average capital employed (ROACE) which are discussed in chapters 22 and 8, respectively.

Game theory

Although strictly not a financial accounting tool, many companies are using game theory and extensions of it to train management to calculate and manage risk situations, for example capital investment risk, pricing strategies, and response to direct competition.

Very similar to war games, the idea is to predict what the 'enemy' might do in a chosen set of circumstances. Game theory is based on a given choice of actions that are determined by the possible alternative actions of an opponent who is playing the same game. Using mathematics and simulation techniques, management can apply a chosen mix of strategies so that whatever the opponent does the opponent cannot do better than to get into a position that you have already worked out and therefore have a counter to.

Game theory is often applied when firms are in direct competition with each other. Examples of game theory application are the price wars that we often see in the newspaper industry, the big oil companies and the travel industry. When a large petrol-producing company lowers the price of petrol, the competition reacts immediately and matches the new price. All these price movements have been strategically calculated to compute how long the firm can keep the price down, what effect it will have on its market share, and how much of that market share increase will be lost when the price goes back up.

Also in game theory a financial model of the competitor firm(s) will be analysed to predict how long, financially, a price war can be sustained. With modern computing power and the involvement of our rocket scientists, these are very serious games, played for high stakes.

17

Sources of Finance

———◇———

COMPANIES *frequently have to raise capital: to replace worn-out fixed assets; to purchase new fixed assets; to finance additional working capital due to an increase in activity; to repay existing debts; to take over other companies; and for many other reasons. The finance industry has developed some very sophisticated financial instruments and sources of finance for organisations to use. In the City, young graduates in mathematics and physics (known in the industry as the 'rocket scientists') are employed to develop these complex new products; here, we'll look only at the most popular and therefore the most commonly used.*

CAPITAL IS OFTEN categorised into short-term, medium- and long-term finance:

▶ short-term finance can be regarded as any liability (debt) repayable within one year, for example a bank overdraft;

▶ medium-term finance is often classified as debts to be repaid within one to ten years;

▶ long-term finance is any debt repayable at some time after ten years.

Prudence and commonsense dictate that short-term finance should only be used for short-term reasons, e.g. stocks, work in progress, debtors, and so on, which may be due to an increase in sales. Medium-term finance should be applied to medium-term situations, e.g. the purchase of fixed assets with a useful life of under ten years. And long-term finance will be invested in long-term assets such as land, factories, plant and machinery and acquisitions having a useful life of ten years or more.

Short-term finance should not be used to finance longer-term investments. Where businesses try and do this, for instance applying a bank overdraft to the purchase of fixed assets, rather than for its proper short-term use in, say, financing working capital, then the overdraft will usually become stuck (becoming hard-core in banking terminology). At this stage, the lending banker will often require the fixed part of the overdraft, i.e. that percentage that does not fluctuate, to be converted into a medium-term loan, thereby adjusting the capital structure of the business to what is financially prudent.

SHORT-TERM FINANCE

Bank overdraft

Probably the most common form of short-term finance is the bank overdraft. It would appear from the media that it is the most unpopular as well. Given a sound case, all the major high street banks and other lenders will be prepared to consider granting an overdraft for a business to finance working capital. Working capital is discussed fully in chapter 9 but, simply put, it is the amount of funds available to a company to meet its short-term liabilities. Often a bank will grant an overdraft to finance the time-lag between sales invoicing and receipt of the money. Overdrafts can also be negotiated to finance stock increases in the busy season of a cyclical business, or indeed just an increase in trade.

Overdrafts are normally sanctioned for one year and re-negotiated annually. They are legally payable on demand, and this is reflected in their short-term treatment in accounts. Banks will charge interest of between 1% and 4% (and sometimes more) above the base rate currently in force, depending on their perception of the risk of lending to that business. Banks may also require to study management accounts (perhaps quarterly or monthly) for companies which appear to be a higher risk, and some may require some form of security, i.e. a charge over some or all of the company's assets and in some cases, for smaller businesses, a charge over the owner's private assets, e.g. taking out a second charge on a house.

The main advantage of an overdraft is that you pay interest only while you have the overdraft, although banks normally also charge an arranging fee. The major disadvantage is that the bank can call in the loan at very little notice – indeed, on demand.

Trade credit

A common financial tool, often used by management, is to negotiate with suppliers preferential trade credit terms, for example paying your suppliers thirty days, sixty days, or more, after receipt of the goods. In some businesses it has become trade custom for suppliers to offer finished goods on a sale-or-return basis, thereby alleviating the suppliers' stock financing costs. (See page 101.)

The purpose of sound trade credit management is to sell your goods or services and collect the money before you have to pay your supplier. This, however, is often only a short-term move, and if you decide to pay your bills sixty days after receipt of invoice instead of the more usual thirty days, you may only be able to do this once. It is, however, very useful for short-term 'overtrading' situations. But care must be taken not to disrupt the good trading relationship you have built up with your suppliers. It is becoming increasingly common for suppliers, as part of their general trading terms and conditions, to charge interest on late payment to counter the loss of interest to them.

Many large companies are blatant in their disregard for the effect that late payment has on small businesses and take a

'Do as you're told' attitude to their suppliers, knowing they have the clout to enforce terms flexible only to them. As a counter to this, the government is discussing proposals for a statutory right to interest on credit.

Invoice discounting

In this instance you sell your debts, i.e. transfer the legal rights in your trade debts, to an invoice-discounting company. In return, the invoice-discounting company will immediately pay you up to say, 80% of the value of your invoices as issued. You still create your own invoices, and have complete control over your accounting function, and receive payments from your customers. However, in most cases you pay your customers' cheques into a nominated account in the invoice-discounting company's name. The balance (20% in our example) – less their charges and commission – is paid to you as soon as you have banked the full invoice amount in that special account.

Obviously the main benefit in using such a service is being paid instantly, and this has no upper limit as the amount is determined by the amounts you are invoicing. By this means, to some extent working capital growth becomes self-financing. This type of financing is 'off balance sheet': in avoiding an overdraft to finance debtors, and growth in debtors, you allow the balance sheet to look more healthy.

Furthermore, this method of discounting your invoices will be unknown to your customers, as they see only your invoices and statements. Because of the charges and administration involved, this type of short-term finance is normally only available to businesses with a substantial turnover. Invoice-discounting companies are often owned by a bank, so advice regarding this service is best sought from your own bank initially.

Factoring

A very similar method of short-term financing is factoring

your debts, commonly known just as 'factoring'. The major difference here is that the factoring company offers a full sales ledger accounting service.

You advise the factoring company whom to invoice and for how much. In return for a management fee, they will create the invoices, maintain the sales ledger, and be responsible for collecting the debts. As part of the service they will normally offer advice on the creditworthiness of your customers. Indeed, the fees they charge will reflect the ability of your customers to pay their debts on time. Again, up to 80% of the value of invoices on approved customers will be payable to you at once. The balance is paid when the factoring company is paid in turn, or to some agreed rolling formula.

Factoring companies maintain that they have become experts in efficient debt-collecting without upsetting their clients' customers. Again, factoring services are only available to companies with substantial turnovers; the factoring charges – similar to those of invoice-discounting – need to be compared with the cost of a bank overdraft plus, of course, the internal cost of running your own sales ledger.

As banks often own their own factoring company, or are in partnership with one, if you wish to factor your debts because you can't obtain an overdraft you may not succeed.

Stock control

Ask any finance directors, and they will agree that stocks are necessary but expensive to finance. A manufacturing company holding three weeks' use of raw materials, two weeks' work in progress, and three weeks' finished goods will need to finance the equivalent of 10% of its annual turnover, just to maintain that stock level. An immediate avenue of short-term finance open to most companies is to reduce stocks at all levels in the organisation and to maintain these lower stock levels. Stock control is examined in chapter 10, but the main point here is that stocks, like debtors, need continual financing and any reduction means cash in the bank.

MEDIUM-TERM FINANCE

Banks

Banks and similar organisations through their business centres specialise in medium-term finance. This might typically be a loan granted for a specific time, at a fixed or variable rate of interest above the base rate. These types of loans should only be used for a specific purpose, such as re-financing the frozen part of an overdraft or the purchase of certain fixed assets. Medium-term loans (MTLs) are more expensive than overdrafts because they are charged on availability, and not on usage only. Fixed-rate MTLs can be more expensive as they seek to reflect, in their repayments, anticipated future movements in interest rate – the lending bank may feel that the base rate is heading upwards over the period of the loan. The main advantages of an MTL is that you know the exact monthly repayments, and when the loan comes to an end; both are useful for financial planning.

Leasing

This is an increasingly popular form of medium-term finance. In a leasing agreement the ownership of an asset remains with the leasing company, but you are entitled to use the asset for a period of time as set out in the leasing agreement, in return for regular set payments, usually monthly. The leasing of motor vehicles, as well as small capital items such as photocopiers, is very common. At the end of the lease period, the asset has to be sold to a third party, although in a lease-purchase agreement you may acquire the asset for a nominal final payment.

Hire purchase

As the name suggests, in a hire purchase agreement (HP) the seller agrees to hire the asset out to the user as laid out in the agreement. The hire and purchase price of the asset, and the interest charge thereon, is usually paid in monthly instalments, over the agreed period of time. At the end of the hire period ownership passes to the hirer. In this instance the asset is shown in the balance sheet at cost; the corresponding HP liability is also shown until it is paid off. The asset will also be depreciated in the normal manner. This reflects 'substance over form': that the 'hidden' reality is one of eventual ownership and this is therefore reflected in the accounts to give a fairer appreciation of the reality. HP agreements are usually expensive but for companies the interest is tax-deductible.

Export finance

Governments have always needed to encourage exporting. Accordingly, the Department of Trade and Industry runs an Export Credits Guarantee Department (ECGD), the job of which is to assist exporters in financing business with overseas buyers. The ECGD has two main roles: to provide exporters with insurance against not being paid due to political and commercial risks, and to assist in the provision of beneficial credit terms to the buyers of UK goods and services overseas. The ECGD runs this service in partnership with the main UK banks, who provide the financing on preferential terms.

LONG-TERM FINANCE

Sale and leaseback

For companies seeking to raise finance, and which own valuable assets such as a factory, office building, land, or a significant industrial plant, sale and leaseback can often be a relatively inexpensive form of long-term finance. Sale and leaseback arrangements release otherwise tied-up capital which can be used to reduce borrowings and/or rolled over to build a new factory, office, plant or whatever without disturbing the present borrowing arrangements. The company seeking finance will negotiate to sell the asset to a specialist company such as an insurance company, or a pension fund. The company will then lease back the asset from the lending company and continue usage as before. In most arrangements of this sort, it is usual for the company now paying a leasing charge to buy back the asset for a nominal sum at the end of the arrangement. These types of transactions are usually completed very quickly and in complete confidence. At the time of writing, it has just been announced that Lloyds of London have entered into such an arrangement for its office building in the City of London.

Mortgages

Mortgages are a widely used source of long-term finance. In the case of a mortgage loan, a single lender will advance a percentage of the value of an asset (e.g. a building) for an agreed period of time, on the specific security of that building. The borrower retains ownership of the asset, subject to a mortgage charge throughout the duration of the loan. Mortgage interest rates can be fixed or variable and are offered by banks, building societies, insurance companies, etc, who will offer both private and commercial transactions. As is now well known to private borrowers, if you fail to keep up mortgage repayments the lender may well invoke their security charge over the asset and force a sale to get their money back.

Venture capital

One of the fastest growing sources of finance for small and medium-sized companies is the venture capital firm. Venture capital is particularly popular for management buy-outs, where the existing management raise capital to buy the business they have effectively been running from its present owners, perhaps a parent company. Venture capital is also used to finance the longer-term expansion of a present business. The venture capital firm will invest in a company that they consider has strong growth potential, so that the risk involved, often high, is balanced by a correspondingly higher rate of return. In most cases the venture capitalist will be looking for a capital gain in the form of a flotation of the client company on the stock market, within, say, three or four years. Venture capital investment is almost always taken in the form of an equity shareholding in the client company of anything between 10% and 49%. Venture capitalists very rarely take control of a client company (i.e. obtain 51% of shareholding) but will usually nominate one or two directors to sit on the board. This is a much closer relationship than is common between other forms of lender and borrower. This hands-on approach means that the venture capitalist will give advice even on the day-to-day running of the business if requested. All the major banks have access to, and will advise on, suitable companies.

The stock market

For many companies the most important step in their development is 'going public': offering their shares for sale on the stock market. This is only available to organisations that have achieved a significant turnover and track record to meet the stringent rules and regulations of obtaining a primary quote on the London Stock Exchange or its little brother AIM (Alternative Investment Market). The reasons that private companies wish to go public are numerous but they will normally revolve around the existing shareholders wishing to sell shares to the public in order to realise funds for their private use, for instance to meet taxes and inheritance tax, or to provide cash for expansion, where other sources of finance cease to be sensible or are too expensive. Going public also has the advantage of making the shares more marketable and thereby often more valuable. The major disadvantage of floating your company on the Stock Exchange is that it is an expensive exercise and fees have to be paid to bankers, accountants, lawyers and underwriters, but existing shareholders will take this into consideration when embarking upon this strategy. The most common methods of raising finance are:

▶ **Offer for sale.** In this case the public are invited to purchase shares, normally at a fixed price; such invitations are published in the press. Following the privatisation issues of the 1980s, most people are aware that new share issues are publicised in newspaper advertisements, and a large percentage of the population now know how to sell shares on the Stock Exchange using a stockbroker or, more commonly, a share shop or bank.

▶ **Rights issue.** For a company already listed on the Stock Exchange, a rights issue is a vehicle that is used to raise further capital from the present shareholders. New ordinary shares or other forms of securities are offered to existing shareholders pro-rata (i.e. 1 for 1) to their current shareholding. In this instance, shareholders can take up their rights to receive new shares or sell the rights on the stock market if the rights have an established value; this is what usually happens as the offer price for the new shares is normally at a discount to what the share price is when the rights issue is made public, so that the shareholders can sell at full price and pocket the difference.

▶ **Private placing.** In some cases a less expensive method of selling, here shares are offered only to a selected number of investors. These investors are pension schemes, fund managers, insurance companies, unit trusts, and so on. Not only cheaper, a private placing is also a quicker and easier route than an open invitation to the public.

MEDIUM-TO LONG-TERM FINANCE

Government and independent sources

There are hundreds of ways companies can seek development finance from government bodies. We have already mentioned export finance, but through the Department of Trade and Industry details can also be obtained of business start-up schemes, Enterprise Zones, government-backed loan schemes, as well as specific grants to deal with particular industry sectors, such as construction and agriculture, and preferential loans for the development of new products which are deemed to be in the national interest. The high street banks can be very helpful here as well as offering advice on which government department to target. There are also independent bodies who can offer advice, such as local Chambers of Commerce, the Institute of Directors, and the professional associations and trade associations, whose local contact numbers can be found in any telephone directory.

Retained profits

Lastly, but just as important as any of the above, are retained profits. When a business is making money, it should set aside a proportion of funds derived from profit each year to provide for expansion of working capital and to partly fund capital expenditure.

18

Directors, Secretaries and Shareholders

———◇———

In OUR EXPERIENCE of running financial training courses, many delegates don't know why their company asks them to follow certain procedures. Often the directors and secretary, responsible to the shareholders, set up procedures designed to meet legal and accounting obligations without explaining the reasons for them to anyone else in the company. This chapter explains the duties and roles which those procedures are designed to support. Managers are increasingly having to make presentations to the Board and it is helpful to know something of your directors' 'angle' on what you are presenting to them, in order to make your presentations more powerful. In addition, you may be appointed to the Board at some time, and it is wise to know what is involved in accepting what is usually seen as a coveted position.

UNDER UK LAW, there are private limited companies and public limited companies; both enjoy the protection of limited liability. This means that the owners of the business – the shareholders – are liable for the liabilities (debts) of the company only up to the amount that they have agreed to pay for their shares in the company. As in nearly all cases shares are issued fully paid, this means in reality that shareholders stand to lose only what they have already invested. Although the laws relating to limited companies are laid down in the Companies Acts, the rules and regulations within each company regarding powers of the directors, rights of the shareholders, and general rules relating to the conduct of the business, are contained in a formal document called the Memorandum and Articles of Association. These clearly state what the company was formed for, and how the company will be governed. Shareholders in general meeting can alter and/or amend the Memorandum and Articles so as to avoid the directors acting outside their powers.

The main differences between a *private limited company* and a *public limited company* are as follows:

▶ a private limited company has 'Limited' at the end of its name;

▶ a public limited company has 'plc' at the end of its name, although it could write the unabbreviated form;

▶ a private limited company can have a sole director;

▶ a public limited company must have at least two directors;

▶ only a public limited company may offer its shares or other stock to the public;

▶ a private limited company can start trading as soon as it is incorporated (formed);

▶ a public limited company must obtain a trading certificate from the Registrar of Companies.

THE BOARD OF DIRECTORS

The company secretary

Every limited company must have a secretary. This individual may not also be the sole director of a private limited company; if there is more than one director then one person may hold both offices. The secretary is responsible for ensuring that the company's statutory books and records are kept up to date – the register of members, register of directors, register of mortgages, the minute book, etc. – and also that all the annual and periodic records as required by the Registrar of Companies are filed correctly, and on time. The secretary also keeps the company seal and signs official documents when the seal is used. The roles and duties of the company secretary vary from one company to another, and will often depend upon the importance put on the position by the directors of the company. In a small firm, the secretary may turn out to be also the accountant, legal adviser, insurance and pension expert, and even personnel officer. In small companies the secretarial functions are often delegated to the companies' external accountants.

In order to avoid a conflict of interest, the secretary's role is normally administrative as opposed to policy-making. In large public companies the position of the company secretary can be very significant, and they may act as a vital continuity link during changes in board membership. In 1992, the Cadbury report on corporate governance commented that: 'All directors should have access to the advice and the services of the company secretary who is responsible to the board of directors for making sure that board procedures are followed, and that applicable rules and regulations are complied with. Any question of the removal of the company secretary should be a matter for the board as a whole.'

Directors

As noted above, a private limited company must have at least one director and a public limited company must have at least two. In theory, directors are appointed by the owners (shareholders) to run the business on their behalf. In reality, the directors are often a self-electing, self-perpetuating body. Shareholders can at any time remove any number of directors and replace them with other people in general meeting.

Normally, however, the directors have enough support from major shareholders to appoint whom they want to see on the board. Appointment to the board of directors is the apex, for many people, of a managerial career.

In the UK's major companies, boards tend to range from between ten and fourteen directors but there is no optimum size that can usefully be used as a benchmark. There are two main types of directors common to UK boards, executive directors and non-executive directors.

Non-executive directors

The role of non-executive directors in large companies would appear to be one of increasing importance, particularly since the publication of the Cadbury report (regarding the responsibilities of executive and non-executive directors) in 1992. Primarily, the non-executive directors are appointed to offer the board objective, independent and expert advice. Most boards will appoint a number of non-executive directors to allow checks and balances upon the executive directors. Current thinking is that *more suitably* qualified and experienced non-executive directors should be appointed than is often the case. Certainly, in times of corporate difficulties, the larger shareholders such as financial institutions, pension-fund managers, and insurance companies, and sometimes even the company's own bankers, may well insist that the board be strengthened by the appointment of non-executive directors with certain types of experience. The Cadbury report recommended that a majority of the non-executive directors should be totally independent, having no business or financial connections with the company. However, once appointed they often tend to acquire share options at very preferential prices, which must water down the degree of independence sought.

Cadbury also recommended that the audit committees, i.e. the internal checking systems, should consist of only non-executive directors. They may obtain – and if necessary demand – free access to all management information to enable them to do their jobs properly. However, in a recent interview which one of the authors conducted with a non-executive director of a major plc, he stated that the most pressing problem was that being part-time he found it difficult to access day-to-day information about the company.

Other roles of the non-executive directors are:

▶ to head the remuneration committee which determines the directors' salaries in as objective a manner as possible; (although, as we read in the papers, many non-executive directors of large companies are often also executive directors of their own company, and these directors sit on each other's remuneration committees);

▶ to bring to the board gaps in expertise in specialist areas such as exploration, environment, international trade;

▶ to make sure that the rights of the shareholders, in particular the minority shareholders, are looked after;

▶ to supervise, in an independent manner, the senior management team (i.e. the executive directors), and to take an objective view on how the company is being run both strategically and regarding its policies;

▶ to seek and obtain independent professional advice at the company's expense if they feel it necessary.

After losses at BP in 1992, it was reported in the press that the non-executive directors were mainly responsible for the removal of the chairman and chief executive. Following this, they split the joint role of chairperson and chief executive into two positions, as recommended in the Cadbury report. In 1993 the non-executive directors of Fison's, on discovering serious trading problems, went to independent financial advisers and were instrumental in getting, in their view, a change in the senior management.

Executive directors

These directors are full-time employees of the company, usually managing directors of the divisions, departmental heads, etc., and as such they actually run the business on a day-to-day basis, within the powers delegated to them by the whole board. In most companies the executive directors are responsible for:

▶ the overall strategy and direction of the organisation;

▶ making sure that the company complies with all legislation, both in the UK and in any other countries where they operate;

▶ ensuring that the company is financially sound, and is able to meet all its obligations and liabilities;

▶ sanctioning all major contracts, such as large capital expenditure programmes;

▶ the introduction and implementation of suitable policies regarding finance, human resources, health and safety at work, etc.;

▶ creating and maintaining suitable organisational structures for the running of the business;

▶ representing the interests of the shareholders and taking note of their views;

▶ (regarding finance:) making sure that suitable accounting policies are applied and are consistent across the whole organisation; making financial judgements and estimates that are reasonable and prudent; stating whether applicable accounting standards have been followed; preparing the financial statements on a 'going concern' basis (see page 23); maintaining proper accounting records for safeguarding the assets of the company; and introducing suitable measures for the prevention of fraud and other irregularities;

▶ safeguarding shareholders' interests with respect to take-overs and mergers;

▶ giving professional advice to other managers in the company, both formally and informally.

Chairperson

The board of directors appoints a chairperson of the board and in some companies this is the most senior position. The chairperson's role, as the name indicates, is to chair the board meetings, and as such that individual fulfils the role of any chair of a meeting. If the chairperson is also the chief executive (although, as we have mentioned, Cadbury recommends the position be split), then this is the most powerful position in the organisation.

It is difficult to set out exactly what a chairperson's role is, as this will vary from company to company, but in most organisations it is to lead the company, acting not only as the figurehead of the organisation but also as the honest broker of the board. As the figurehead, this is often the person who fronts the organisation, speaks in public on behalf of the company, acts as the ambassador of the company, and deals with the large institutional shareholders. In many large companies, these individuals become well known to the public – Rupert Murdoch, Alan Sugar, and Anita Roddick are three who spring to mind.

Chief executive

Again, it is very difficult to state exactly the duties and responsibilities of the chief executive. In organisational theory, every company needs one person who takes the final decisions, and acts as the team leader of the board. Functional directors – those who, on a day-to-day basis, run divisions, sites, departments – need to have a colleague to whom they can turn for advice as well as seeking information about the overall picture of the business. The chief executive fulfils these and other roles and is the coordinator and leader for the directors. The chief executive takes the highest risk and for that reason is normally paid the most. These days being chief executive can be a very precarious life; the London Stock Exchange, for example, has lost two chief executives in three years.

THE SHAREHOLDERS

Owners of companies, called shareholders, can be people or some other form of legal entity, e.g. another company. Shareholders can own shares singly or with other people, and have statutory rights as set out in the Companies Acts. As a summary, shareholders have the following rights:

▶ to have their ownership of shares in a company acknowledged by their entry in the register of members;

▶ to be invited to and to attend general meetings of the company, e.g. the annual general meetings;

▶ at such general meetings, to speak, ask questions and vote on resolutions put to them by the chair of the meeting;

▶ to appoint a proxy to attend general meetings and give authority for that proxy to vote on the shareholder's behalf;

▶ within the rules as set out in the Memorandum and Articles of Association, to call with other shareholders an extraordinary general meeting of the company to vote on resolutions on specific issues;

▶ to be informed and if necessary consulted on any changes to the constitution of the company, e.g. to increase the number of directors.

The Cadbury report suggested that while there are sound commercial reasons for the directors to run the company and make all the important decisions (in particular takeovers and mergers), it should be recognised by boards of directors that there are occasions when such important matters should be brought to the attention of shareholders.

Although it may, at first, seem unreasonable that the owners of the company don't have the right to peruse its day-to-day management figures, a moment's reflection will see that this is sensible: it would not be wise for one company to give all its confidential trading information to a competitor simply because that competitor owns one share in that company, purchased on the open-market Stock Exchange. Directors alone have that information. When they abuse it, they occasionally make the headlines and spend a little time residing at Her Majesty's pleasure.

Although, legally, shareholders own the company, in larger companies with a large number of shareholders, power will reside with blocks of shareholders (institutions such as pension funds and insurance companies). These institutional shareholders, because of the block holdings, do influence the directors of companies and indeed the outcome of events. In 1996 the fiercely fought takeover battle between Forte and Granada was influenced by one fund management company which owned over 15% of the shares in both Forte and Granada. When shareholders at the annual general meeting of British Gas in 1995 wanted to decrease the salary of the then chief executive, Cedric Brown, they were defeated by the chairman of the company, holding enough proxies granted to him by the institutional shareholders to vote against the resolution.

Because of their size of shareholdings, these institutions are often fêted and courted by companies who give them presentations on performance and future plans, site and factory visits, and the 'corporate hospitality' they can offer. This means that the financial institutions get company information that is not made available to the smaller shareholders.

One interesting development of recent years is the concept of ethical shareholdings. Here, small pressure groups of shareholders do seem to be able to put leverage on directors not to invest in, say, totalitarian regimes or companies which pollute the environment. There are also investment companies which aim to channel their funds only into genuinely ethical investments.

Companies are intended to be run on democratic lines; in practice, that means that despite the will of a large number of people, under the present rules, boards of directors who own (or have under their control) 51% of the shares are able to do as they wish.

19

Audits

———◇———

"BRIAN", the son of the managing director of a large manufacturing company, was partly drunk and totally relaxed as he danced with a young woman his age in the disco. He naturally wanted to impress her and told her a number of humorous stories about his father's business acumen. There was the fact that the company was paying for half a million pounds worth of personal assets on the family farm; there was the story about money privately withdrawn from the company in the guise of 'contractor payments'; and he particularly liked the one about how stock values were twice what they should be and 'the auditors haven't got a chance of finding out'. When he related the story to us, he did not reveal his success that night, but he was honest enough to admit that the next time he met the woman the conversation was less light-hearted. At his father's premises she shook his hand and introduced the members of her audit team.

Your company may see the auditors only once a year; or they may seem to be permanently in residence. This chapter explains what they are up to.

LARGE COMPANIES exceeding a given turnover limit are subject to audit requirement. The audit is an examination of the books and records supporting the company's accounts. It is conducted by an authorised auditor: a member of the qualified accountancy profession registered for audit. The purpose of the audit is basically to report to shareholders on the activities of the directors.

It is the directors who are legally responsible for the maintenance of proper books of accounts and the subsequent preparation of accounts based on those books. They may delegate that work, often to professional accountants, but they retain the legal responsibility. The auditors are therefore reporting on the degree to which the directors have discharged their duties properly.

Until recently, the audit requirement applied almost without modification to all companies of whatever size, but was more recently lifted from smaller companies on the basis that in many of those companies the shareholders and directors were in fact the same people (particularly in family companies) or that there were other governing constraints such as the requirements of banks which would be able to insist on certain reporting and external verifications by audit firms if they so required. There is an interim stage between those small companies needing no verifications whatsoever and the full audit requirement of large companies; here a report by accountants, but not a full audit, is required.

Assuming the auditors have reason to believe that the directors have discharged their duties properly and published proper accounts based on well maintained books and records, they will issue a 'clean' audit report which will form part of the statutory records lodged at Companies House. If the auditors find that the accounts are not properly constructed they have a duty in law to point this out in their audit report. In addition, they must quantify the distortion and, where appropriate, comment on the effects on the disclosed profit, assets, and so on.

In order to fulfil their duties, the auditors approach the examination in several ways. These are the areas in which you, as a manager, are likely to encounter your company's auditors.

1 They will examine the systems at work in the company. This may entail flowcharting the systems so that they are aware of all document flows relating to financial matters within the company. Any potential distortions or errors caused, or likely to arise, by the systems must be pointed out to the directors. If the auditors have reason to feel

that actual distortions have occurred, this must be reported.

2   The auditors must test the systems to ensure that they are functioning correctly; that they are capable of producing reliable documentation; and that they in fact *do* produce reliable documentation. Statistically calculated samples within the system are tested to ensure compliance with internal procedures; for example, whether there have been two signatories on cheques over certain amounts; whether there has been restriction of payment to creditors based on an agreed authorisation procedure; and so on.

3   They will carry out certain testing of source documents through the system to ensure mathematical precision is maintained. The number of documents that need to be examined will depend on the type and complexity of the company.

4   They will fully test and examine any area where there is a potential for substantial error. For example, if a company has purchased a very large fixed asset or number of fixed assets, the auditors may decide that it is important to examine all those rather than a statistical sample, and perhaps follow it through to an examination of the physical assets themselves.

5   They will seek to verify the assets listed in the balance sheet: ensuring that fixed assets exist and are of the value stated; that investments are properly held in the company's name; that debtors are capable of realising their stated value or that the bad debt provision is adequate to meet expected needs; that stocks have been sensibly and consistently valued and that write-downs are appropriate and justifiable; that bank accounts are held in the company's proper name; and so on.

The auditors will seek to verify as much as possible of the company's documentation against external documentation. They will, for example, reconcile the company's cash books to the bank statements received from the bank, this external source providing some confirmation to the auditors that the books are correct. Similarly, the auditors may write to a statistical sample of debtors asking them to confirm to the company that the balance the company believes it is owed by them is the same as in their own books. There may be a similar circularisation to creditors, to check amounts that the company owes.

Inevitably, the audit requirement means that there will be auditors operating within large companies almost continuously, and indeed in some companies they are present throughout the year. Their relationship must be one of as much independence as possible, given that they are working in close contact with those that they are in effect 'policing'.

The selection of auditors by the board of directors can clearly lead to a dilution of this independence. Auditors are in practice selected by the very people on whom they will be reporting. Although the appointment of auditors is ratified by the shareholders at the annual general meeting, the reality is that in many cases the directors' choice is unchallenged. However, the professional ethics of the auditing companies and their governing bodies provide for maintained independence.

Companies hold what are sometimes known as 'beauty contests' in order to select auditors, for a variety of reasons. Because of cost-cutting, and given the size of the fees involved, large companies will invite the three or four major players to tender for the audit. To make meaningful tenders the auditing firms must be granted a walk-through the business to assess the work. They then submit their tenders and make presentations to the audit committee of the board, who will recommend which audit firm the board should appoint. These 'beauty contests' are also used when a company needs to change its auditors; typically, this can arise when your auditor is also the auditor of a new major competitor.

Multinational companies are likely to prefer an audit firm that is represented in the countries they operate in, or seek to expand into; this saves money and time, and often leads to useful introductions.

Companies increasingly look towards their auditing firms to provide a wider range of services than the accountancy, tax and audit that was the staple diet of some years ago. Audit firms now often have related 'arms' which can offer management consultancy services, and so on.

Joint audits are now becoming more common, particularly with overseas divisions of companies. Many companies find themselves in partnership, in some activities, with companies with whom they are in other ways in competition (e.g. BP and Mobil linked up for certain operations in 1996). The partnership will want a representation from the joint auditors of both companies' audit firms.

20

Intangible Assets

———◇———

The value of tangible fixed assets and current assets can fairly easily be determined and agreed, usually because a certain amount of money has been spent on them, or they are some form of money themselves. The value of intangible assets, however, is open to debate. For some companies, by far their most important asset can be goodwill, a brand name or some other intangible asset. Intangible assets have a value, earn income for the company and for this reason are a commodity bought and sold in the marketplace. This chapter describes some of the types of intangible asset you may find entered in a company's balance sheet.

Brand names

IF WE consider a brown fizzy liquid, sweet to the taste, made up of vegetable flavourings and water, with gas added, it may not appear to be the most exciting product; but to marketing and sales people the mere mention of the name Coca-Cola brings tears to their eyes. It has been nearly one hundred years, so the story goes, since addictive cocaine was put into Coca-Cola but it is still the largest selling brand of soft drink in the world. For this reason the manufacturers spend millions of dollars in worldwide advertising to promote their extraordinarily powerful brand name. The Coca-Cola name and logo is still the best known of all product logos worldwide. In 1995 a UK supermarket chain had to change its own Cola brand packaging because it was threatened with court action on the grounds that shoppers might well mistake it for 'The Real Thing'.

Goodwill

Non-financial management often regard the concept of 'goodwill' as an accountant's trick (a 'creative accounting' technique) to value a company for more than what it is really worth. Nothing could be further from the truth. At its simplest, goodwill is the difference between, on the one hand, the value of the tangible assets less liabilities, and, on the other, what the company is being valued at, or what the owners of the company are prepared to sell the business for.

Goodwill represents the history, the good name and the reputation of the business in the marketplace. A company may have built up a customer or client list which the would-be purchaser of the business would like to acquire; the working relationship with those clients represents a component of goodwill. The valuation of goodwill can involve a very complicated formula regarding sales trends, repeat business, advertising impact, and so on. A good example of goodwill concerns Harrods. Harrods is a powerful brand name, but it is more than that because the store sells many items of other people's brand names. The 'goodwill' of Harrods is a history of service, quality, reputation. Any would-be buyer of Harrods would have to pay a significant premium over the asset value of the store and the stock in it, to 'acquire' the reputation that draws customers from all over the world.

Goodwill is, of course, just as important to smaller organisations. A firm of accountants wishing to sell their business to another accounting firm would normally be asking for a substantial premium over and above the assets of the business. This goodwill premium represents a value put on the client list as built up by the firm over the years. (If the client list includes special people, for example royalty, then no doubt the value of the goodwill increases.) However, part of the valuation depends on the client/accountant relationship being ongoing, i.e. guaranteed repeat business – that guarantee has value.

As a would-be purchaser of this accounting firm, you

would only be willing to pay for those clients who, you can be reasonably certain, will remain with you. For this reason it is not uncommon these days for deals to be struck on the basis of a percentage of goodwill, relating to the current client list, being paid straight away, the balance to be paid at a later date when the historical accounts show what percentage of clients remained with the new firm. Consideration must also be given to the client mix, i.e. the percentages of clients with turnovers under and over certain levels; the degrees of risk (for insurance purposes) of the nature of the client's business; and factors regarding local competition, growth of the local area, etc. We interviewed a private dentist on the subject of goodwill, who suggested that how long his filling and repair work lasted was probably his patients' definition of value for money and hence, in the long run, goodwill (and continued loyalty).

Transfer of goodwill can be a problem, however. A sole trader, such as a carpenter or jobbing builder, may well have built up a great deal of goodwill over a number of years in the local community. This goodwill is more difficult to transfer to another person (and therefore to sell) because clients are 'buying the person', and when he or she leaves they feel free to make new relationships. The sole trading entity is difficult to 'pass on'.

In accounting, we tend to recognise two different aspects of goodwill: goodwill that is purchased from another party, and goodwill that is self-generated by the business. Purchased goodwill is usually written off (i.e. gradually reduced in value to zero by charging a notional 'cost' to the profit and loss account each year) over (usually) three years, on the basis that after three years any goodwill with clients can reasonably be regarded as due to your own relationships with them. Where goodwill is self-generated, the Accounting Standards Board advises that any expenditure used to create goodwill, e.g. advertising and promotion, should be written off to the profit and loss account, as incurred.

The value to the business of its goodwill is therefore not generally recognised as an asset in the balance sheet. This, of course, creates the strange nature of the animal, in that it is resurrected only at a time of takeover, merger or sale of the business. In other words, throughout the ongoing life of the business it has, and generates, goodwill but this is recognised as an asset of value only when there is a change in ownership.

The most obvious proof of the hidden value of goodwill is the effect of losing it. Hoover – which in the English language is still synonymous with vacuum cleaners – created significant goodwill over a number of decades through reliable products and innovative advertising (the authors can still remember the Hoover jingle from decades ago: 'A Hoover beats, as it sweeps, as it cleans.'). However, a few years ago, purchasers of Hoover products of over £100 were offered two *free* return flights to the USA; not surprisingly, the take-up was immense, and Hoover – by insisting on adherence to a strict set of rules and regulations concerning the offer – upset a large number of customers, who did not obtain their free flights. Goodwill was lost and Hoover mounted a rescue policy – in effect rescuing its own goodwill that had been damaged by one mistake.

Equally famous was the unfortunate statement by Gerald Ratner, made presumably tongue-in-cheek, that one of his product-lines was 'crap'. The comment, made to a group of businessmen at a conference, was highly publicised and resulted in the almost total loss of goodwill in the Ratner name.

Patents

A patent is granted by the government to assure an inventor of the sole right to make, use and sell the invention, for a limited period. Patents can also be granted on developments if the developer can convince the Patent Office that what they have created has the status of an invention. The laws relating to patents date back as far as the seventeenth century. Hundreds of patents are applied for and taken out monthly by individuals, small businesses and large organisations, who wish to protect something they have invented and/or developed. By taking out a patent on new products, processes, machines, etc., the patentee is in effect ring-fencing an area of technology and/or development with the warning that any person or company copying it will be, or can be, prosecuted. The prime purpose of a patent is to protect the inventor, for a given number of years, so that for a period following the effort (and expense) of creating something new, that individual or organisation has the sole right to make money from their own efforts.

Patents can be taken out in the UK, Europe, the USA, and to some extent worldwide. However, their effectiveness is dependent on the ability and/or willingness of companies and countries to enforce the patent laws and agreements through the courts. Not all countries subscribe to international patent agreements and as the patentee often has to make full disclosure concerning the invention, process or whatever, there is an inherent risk of someone else exploiting the invention from a country where they can be reasonably sure they will not be prosecuted.

Patent law is complex, and any individual or organisation wishing to file a patent application should seek advice from a registered patent agent. A list of these can be obtained from the United Kingdom Patent Office and the European Patent Office.

Licensing

Once a patent has been granted, the owner can exploit it in various ways for the length of the patent period. Instead of using it as a fence to keep out the competition, the patentee may decide to exploit it by allowing one or more people and/or organisations to use it for a limited period in return for an agreed licence fee. This licensing operation – in its simplest form – is an undertaking by the owner of the patent not to sue the licensee for patent infringement so long as the licensee complies with all the terms and conditions of the licence. Such licence agreements may often stipulate in which countries the licensee can operate and may even state quotas of, say, production units that the licensee is required to produce, or not allowed to exceed.

If the granters of the licence agree not to issue any other licences and also not to use the invention themselves, this is known as an *exclusive licence*. If they contract to grant no further licences but do not exclude themselves from exploiting the invention, the licence is known as a *sole licence*.

Reasons for granting a licence are varied, but usually a licence is issued where the patentee has not got the financial strength to fully exploit the invention, economically and/or geographically; they will therefore enter into a 'partnership agreement' with other companies which can maximise sales. Selling the licence for a lump sum or on a royalty basis means that the patentee can fully exploit the economic benefits of the invention for the term of the patent.

Countries often restrict the sale of sensitive technology licences to some countries if they don't wish them to have access to the technology. 'UK plc' is a substantial inventor of technology and processes, and exports licences to the emerging countries, in particular, the fast-growing market areas of the Far East. Some people comment that selling such licences is the same as selling the family silver, and is short-termism; usually the inventor is wishing to maximise the benefits of the invention in the legally granted timeframe.

Trademarks

Trademarks and tradenames are very similar to patents, in that they can be protected by registering them with the Registrar of Trademarks. If an organisation builds up a reputation using a tradename and/or a trademark (which is often also a brand name, as described above) then by registering it they ensure that nobody else is able to use that name or mark. The owner of the name or mark can sue anyone or any organisation using the name or mark – or indeed a similar name or mark that may confuse the general public. To prevent having to argue whether a name or mark falls into this latter category, similar-sounding names or marks can be protected: Marks and Spencer plc has allegedly registered 'Marks and Sparks' as one of its tradenames.

The Companies Act 1985 allows companies to show brand names, patents, licences, tradenames and trademarks in the balance sheet. Such intangible assets can be identified (as assets) whether they were purchased or were created by the company itself.

It is in any company's interest to place as high a value as possible on all intangible assets, including goodwill, so that a would-be purchaser would have to pay a higher price. Indeed, one of the standard defences against the takeover or sale of a business is to revalue all its assets, including the intangibles, at as high a price as possible.

21

The Role of Depreciation

———◇———

IF YOU ARE a manager in charge of a whole category of fixed assets, for example, company plant and machinery, the car fleet, the computer systems, and so on, you will have to provide the finance department with estimates of the cost of using those assets – for which no money will actually flow – based on many factors relating to the assets and the company's use of them. This chapter sets out the basis of the information the finance department will need from you, and what considerations you should bring to bear on valuing the diminution in value of the assets in your charge.

In some cases the manufacturer of the asset will offer an 'expected life'; but you are cautioned to consider their estimate on the basis of your usage. Sometimes the manufacturer can provide useful data based on experience from your competitors.

ASSET OR STOCK?

WHEN a company buys an item, its accounting treatment of the item will depend basically on three factors:

1　the purpose for which the item was purchased;

2　the expected life of the item;

3　the cost.

Based on these criteria, certain items are regarded as long-term, or fixed, assets. If the purpose of the item is to resell it, then regardless of cost or expected life the item is not a fixed asset but rather a part of stock, or in certain circumstances could be deemed to be held as an investment. However, if the purpose of the item is to use it in the furtherance of the company's normal activities, then it may qualify to be regarded as a fixed asset. If we take the example of a company which manufactures and sells computers, its fixed assets might be:

▶ company cars which are not bought for resale but to provide the sales force with transport so that they can travel around the country making sales of computers;

▶ machinery on which the components of the computer are produced and on which the computers themselves are assembled;

▶ the building, factory and offices, in which the operation is undertaken.

The expected life of the item plays a part here. If, say, a piece of machinery is expected to last less than a year before wearing out, becoming obsolete or being replaced for some other reason, it would not be capitalised as a fixed asset but would be written off as a cost of that year in the profit and loss account. An item is considered a fixed asset if its expected life is at least more than one year.

So, given the first two criteria, we see that fixed assets are generally assets which are used in the furtherance of the business and which have an expected long-term life (i.e. at least more than one year). The third criteria, cost, is one only of materiality. It may be that the accounts department buys calculators for £5 which are used in the furtherance of the business and which have an expected life of several years; but due to their very small cost these would probably be written off in the year of purchase rather than capitalised into the future.

Any computers which our computer-manufacturing

company bought for resale would not be regarded as fixed assets but would be regarded as *stock*. On the other hand, customers who bought its computers to use in the further-ance of their activities and with an expected long-term life, would regard those computers as their *fixed assets*. The nature of the item itself is not a criterion for choosing whether or not a particular asset should be regarded as a fixed asset.

PROVIDING FOR DEPRECIATION

Although the expected life of the asset within the company is regarded as long-term, almost all assets have a finite life and will eventually be useless for a number of reasons, as set out below. The depreciation charge is a transfer from the opening balance sheet value to the profit and loss account at the close of each year. The aim of providing for depreciation is to charge to the profit and loss account in each year the true value of *using* the fixed assets in the business for that year. While this seems simple at first sight, it is in fact not only highly complex but generally accepted as impossible. In practice, therefore, the provision for depreciation is a policy of combining past experience, forward planning and expec-tation.

The one exception to this principle is land, which is gener-ally regarded as an appreciating asset – its value *increases* over time – and is therefore not subject to depreciation in the accounts. (This special situation arises because of the combi-nation of scarcity, arising from fixed supply, and ever-increasing demand. 'Buy land,' said Mark Twain. 'They've stopped making it.')

The reasons for the eventual uselessness of an asset, and the methods of calculating depreciation appropriately, are summarised over the following pages.

1   Wear and tear

All assets wear out over time, due to friction, metal fatigue, rust, rot, decay, exposure to the elements and a whole variety of other reasons.

Calculation

At best, you can only *estimate* the length of time before a given asset will wear out. Two identical desks or filing cabinets purchased on the same day will not wear out at the same rate. How they are used, where they sit, and the care taken of the furniture by their individual keepers will all make a difference. However, even if the wear and tear on each desk or filing cabinet could be individually calculated, it would be an absurd level of complexity for the company to charge depreciation asset by asset, and even then it would still be only an estimation.

Cars have a generally expected average useful life of some three to four years, from a corporate point of view, before they should be replaced. The nature of the use of a car makes its eventual decay into uselessness inevitable. But some assets cannot offer any help to estimators. One of our client companies, a textile manufacturing factory in the North of England, is still using the same equipment that it has used for the past 150 years. Even the incredibly optimistic, technological Victorians could hardly have anticipated that!

Becoming uneconomical and/or unreliable

Some assets can be predicted to need replacement after a given period of time not because they will wear out completely by then, but because their deterioration is such that the cost of repair and maintenance outweighs the cost of replacement. The car is a good example: after three or four years it may well still have a useful life but the costs of maintenance and repair each subsequent year may be more than the finance costs of purchasing a new car. In addition, the older a vehicle gets the less reliable it may be and this may be an unacceptable risk to the company. Delivery vans which break down not only waste time but annoy customers and possibly lose long-term customer loyalty.

Calculation

Again, an *estimate* is the best you can do.

3 Obsolescence

An item may become obsolete even though it is in perfect working condition and could continue for many years with the same efficiency as in the past. For example, many of the printing presses housed in Fleet Street could well have gone on for many years but became obsolete because technology had created a new way of printing, via computer technology. Computers themselves almost always tend to become obsolete before they wear out as the pace of development of technology, driven by increasingly complex computer programs, means that companies must replace their computers in order to keep ahead of, or at least level with, their competitors. With the increasing pace of information technology and global communications, almost any equipment within that field is prone to possible obsolescence, virtually without warning. It has been suggested, for example, that even the massive global investment in land-line telecommunications (i.e. the telephone plugged into the wall) could be made obsolete by the expected massive expansion in cellular technology where everyone will eventually carry a personal telephone on them at all times with no need for land-linked technology whatsoever.

Calculation

There is a growing case for writing off, as a short-term asset, almost any computer hardware or software, on the basis that development is at such a pace that virtually everything is becoming obsolete within a twelve-month period.

4 Inadequacy

An item may become inadequate even though it is in perfect working condition and is not regarded as obsolete. For example, a small removals company with a number of transit vans all in good condition and as up-to-date as available, may make changes in its activity which mean the vans become inadequate and will have to be disposed of. If the company finds it is increasingly moving into larger bulk transportation then it will need to buy much larger lorries and the transit vans may simply be unable to contribute to the new work.

Calculation

Most companies have some reasonable plan of what they expect to achieve over the medium term: say, five years. On this basis you should be able to predict to some degree whether or not you expect your assets will become inadequate. However, all companies also face the challenge of change and have to be equipped to deal with surprise inadequacies and replacement needs.

5 Depletion

Certain specialised assets, called *wasting assets*, have finite lives due to their inherent nature. For example, a gold mine is a fixed asset but its value will deplete gradually as the gold in it is extracted.

Calculation

It is often difficult to estimate the total mineral wealth contained in a mine; it is therefore difficult to estimate the life of this sort of asset, although some reasonable estimate can and must be made. However, the equation changes with the onset of technology. There comes a point with a mine when the extraction of the remaining mineral is not economical and the mine generally closes with a quantity still available for, but uneconomical for, extraction. However, if at some time in the future technological changes make extraction cheaper, then what appears now to be a residual level may become an economic proposition again. The combination of these uncertainties makes this calculation no more than an *estimate*.

6 Expiry

Certain assets have a finite life for legal or contractual reasons. For example, a company might buy a licence to sell another company's products for a limited period, say, a five-year licence. After the five-year period the company no longer has the right to make those sales, or will have to re-negotiate a new licence. The original licence is therefore an asset with a fixed life of five years. A lease is a very common fixed asset of this kind.

Calculation

In the case of fixed-term contracts, leases, and so on, you have the closest to an actual depreciation per year that you are likely to meet. A twenty-year royalty agreement can be written off in twenty equal instalments until it is regarded as having no value in twenty years' time, which precisely matches the reality. In truth, the royalty agreement probably has greater value in its early years than its later years but it will be difficult to predict this. Conversely, changes in fashion trends and popularity (if, for example, you had the royalty agreement to sell the records of a particular performing artist) could mean that in the later years when you expected there to be little interest in sales you could be holding the contract for the Number One performing artist of that time. So in reality the year-on-year charge may not reflect the actual change in value per year. But at least it does bring us to the correct end valuation, i.e. nil.

Terminology

Your accounting department may use different wording to describe depreciation of certain classes of assets. For example, while the term *depreciation* generally applies to the first four classes of assets described above, *provision for depletion* is the usual term for wasting assets and *amortisation* for writing down assets such as leases. These are all forms of depreciation.

A note about appreciation

There are certain assets, even within classes normally regarded as depreciating, which may in fact appreciate, i.e. increase in value over time. Cars, for example, generally depreciate but classic cars, or collectable cars, appreciate. Generally speaking, appreciation is ignored in accounts (on the basis of conservatism – see chapter 3). There is provision for the appreciation of land and buildings by periodic revaluation, though in most cases this is recognition of the increase in value of the land rather than the building.

Closing value

The calculation of depreciation has one further significant variable that can only be estimated. That is the value of the asset at the end of its expected life. You might purchase a car for, say, £18,000 and estimate that it has an expected life of three years. On a simple basis, you would therefore write off £6,000 per year for three years. But although you will have written the car off to a nil value it will in fact have some residual value (a sales, trade-in or even scrap value). It is unlikely that you can predict what that is with any accuracy. Market forces, fashions, the state of the car, and so on, will all be factors three years ahead, for which you can only make a guess at the present time.

What does depreciation mean?

The word *depreciation* has three possible meanings:

1 **A decrease in value.** Between two dates a particular asset will reduce in value and depreciation is the calculation of that decrease.

2 **Replacement shortfall.** If the new asset to replace the one depreciated costs the same as the one it is replacing when it was initially bought, then depreciation is the calculation of the shortfall between the residual sale price of the first asset and the amount needed to replace it new. In times of inflation, with initial cost prices increasing, the shortfall is always likely to be greater than the depreciation charge. For example, if you buy an asset for £10,000 and depreciate it over four years to a residual value of nil, you will have a depreciation charge of £10,000; if the replacement cost is £12,000, the shortfall (the difference between £12,000 and nil) is also £12,000.

3 **Allocation of cost.** This is the basis of the accounting treatment of depreciation. It transfers the reduction in value of the balance sheet asset to the profit and loss account, i.e. charging the cost of using the asset to the profit and loss account for that year to reflect usage of that asset for the year.

CALCULATING DEPRECIATION

There are two main methods in use:

The straight-line method

This charges an equal amount of depreciation for each year over the expected life of the asset. For example, if the asset cost £10,000, is estimated to have a residual value of £2,000 and will therefore depreciate over, say, four years by a total of £8,000, then £2,000 will be charged to the profit and loss account in each of the four years during which the asset is in use. The straight-line percentage is therefore 25% per annum of the total depreciation.

Reducing balance

This method is designed to reflect the fact that most assets lose the greatest value in their earliest years, and 'weights' the depreciation more heavily to those early years in an attempt to reflect as near to 'actual' loss in value as possible. Using the same asset (with the same expected life and residual value) as in the example above, the reducing balance percentage would be approximately 33%, calculated as follows:

Initial cost:	£10,000	Year 1	33% (£3,300)	Value carried forward £6,700
		Year 2	33% (£2,211)	Value carried forward £4,489
		Year 3	33% (£1,481)	Value carried forward £3,007
		Year 4	33% (£992)	Residual value £2,015

There is a third alternative used in certain rarer circumstances:

The revaluation method

This method is applied by companies with large numbers of small-value assets with long-term life. For example, an engineering company may have thousands of bits of engineering tools and so on. It is not possible to estimate their individual life, since many will be damaged or lost throughout the year.

The revaluation method therefore takes the valuation of all the assets at the beginning of the year, adds the value of purchases of fixed assets of that category during the year and then does a similar 'fixed assets stock check' at the end of the year. The difference between the opening figure plus purchases and the closing figure is therefore regarded as the depreciation charge for the year. We stress that this is a much rarer method, used in specialist circumstances.

THE FINAL RECKONING

Throughout this chapter we have been considering depreciation as an estimation, and have explained the reasons why this should be. However, if these estimates were to go unchecked then over many years the accounts would gradually become increasingly less accurate. The adjustment that rectifies this and brings the eventual total charge to the profit and loss account to an accurate one comes when the asset is disposed of. The actual proceeds received from the sale, or the nil proceeds in the result of scrapping of an asset, are set against the written-down value at that time and any adjustment carried to the profit and loss account as a profit or loss on disposal of asset.

For example, take the asset which you purchased for £10,000 and wrote down at a rate of 25% straight-line per annum. You would start the fourth year with the asset valued at £10,000 less £6,000, giving a written-down value of £4,000. Let us assume that you sold it in that year for £2,500. The difference of £1,500 would be written off as a loss on disposal of asset in that year's profit and loss account. The total charge for depreciation over the period for which you had the asset would therefore be £7,500, i.e. the difference between the cost and eventual selling price of the asset. Were you to scrap it that year for no proceeds it would come into the fourth year at a value of £4,000 and you would carry a loss of £4,000 to the profit and loss account for that year. The total charge would therefore be the £10,000 over the four-year period. In each case, the actual total depreciation charge differs from the £8,000 expected at the start, but the difference is accounted for at the time of asset disposal.

If an asset is retained beyond its expected life, as will often happen, it is usually carried in the balance sheet as a nominal £1 value, simply to recognise its existence. On eventual disposal, again, any residual profit or loss is charged to that year's profit and loss account. In the case of the above asset, let us suppose you kept it far beyond the expected life. It is held in the balance sheet for £1 and some eight years after you originally purchased it, all of its value having been written off in the first five years at £2,000 p.a., you then find that you can dispose of it to a scrap merchant for £50. The resultant profit on disposal of asset, £49, would be carried to the profit and loss account.

A FINAL WORD FROM THE TAX OFFICE ...

The above explanations show how depreciation is usually an estimation and one where the accuracy will only be computed at the point of eventual disposal. Since the depreciation charge is a transfer from the opening balance sheet value to the profit and loss account for that year, by varying our depreciation policy we can effectively manipulate our profit for the year.

For example, if you have a profit from trading of £80,000 before depreciation, and your depreciation policy results in a transfer of depreciation to the profit and loss account for that year of £20,000, then your resultant profit is £60,000. However, with exactly the same trading activity but with a different depreciation policy, you might find that you should charge the profit and loss account £50,000, and your profit is now halved to £30,000.

Needless to say, the Inland Revenue are not predisposed to

allowing companies or individuals to effectively set their own tax charge. For taxation purposes, therefore, depreciation is ignored, i.e. added back to the profit and loss account, so that the base calculation of taxable profit in the above example would be the £80,000 of pre-depreciation profit (subject to other rules and regulations affecting the adjustment of accounts profit to tax profit). For tax purposes, the Inland Revenue allows all companies the same percentage of depreciation, known as *capital allowances*, to cover replacement of assets, thereby providing a measure of equality and regulation. At the time of writing (1996) the basic capital allowance rate is fixed at 25% per annum, calculated by the reducing balance method.

22

Capital Expenditure

⟨⟩

NON-FINANCIAL MANAGERS *often get into major disagreement with financial managers in their demands for capital expenditure. These relate to assets which represent significant commitment on the part of the company. Often large amounts of money are involved, and all applications have to be fully worked through and documented. This chapter sets out the considerations and the presentations that will be needed to justify such requests, so that you can set out your proposals in a way that will get results (or at least explain why you have to go without).*

CAPITAL EXPENDITURE, often abbreviated to 'Capex', is the amount of money committed to create, replace, add to, or improve, existing fixed assets, e.g. land and buildings, vehicles, plant and equipment.

Companies finance capital expenditure out of profits, borrowings, or raising capital from shareholders. The collective Capex decisions of businesses within the UK obviously have a significant influence on the overall growth of the economy, as this type of capital formation increases the country's ability to produce more goods and services, or at least to continue to produce at current levels. In many discussions of short-termism it is alleged that in comparison to Germany the UK businesses do not invest enough in Capex and distribute too much money by way of dividends instead. Certainly in times of financial difficulty many UK companies have cut back capital budgets to conserve cash. In the long run, however, capital, i.e. money for assets is necessary for survival.

When any firm or organisation makes a decision to invest in assets, it incurs a current cash outlay for benefits to be yielded in the future. It is for this reason that Capex decisions are normally judged by the rate of the expected return on investment (ROI), and most companies have clear and set criteria that Capex proposals must satisfy before the money is sanctioned.

Capex is expenditure on an asset that will last longer than one year. As mentioned in previous chapters, when a company incurs a cost that transaction has to be recorded in the books of account and will end up either in the profit and loss account or in the balance sheet. Any amount of money spent that is used up immediately, e.g. gas, salaries, telephone, etc., is written off to the profit and loss account; whereas money spent to purchase or improve a fixed asset will be 'capitalised' – i.e. shown in the 'assets' section of the balance sheet.

Normally, expenditure should comply with the following in order to be regarded as capital expenditure:

1 It must be for a *material amount*. There is very little point in regarding small purchases as assets even if they do last longer than one year. Depreciating an asset of say £100 or under would be time-wasting in accounting terms. The size of the company and its 'usual' levels of transactions will determine the appropriate 'cut-off' level for this decision.

2 The asset must have a *life expectancy of more than one year*. Any assets with a life expectancy of one year or less should be written off to the profit and loss account, whatever their value.

3 Similarly, the asset must have *some value after a year*. Its existence alone is not the only factor to consider. For example, the old-style space programme rockets (one-off use) may still exist, technically, in orbit, but they can never be reused and would have to have been written off in the year of launch. On the other hand, the reusable

space shuttle has an ongoing life, with genuine value, and would be regarded as capital in nature.

The cost of using an asset (its depreciation) is charged on a 'writing down' basis to the profit and loss account (see chapter 21).

With improvements to assets, sometimes it is difficult to establish if the expenditure is true Capex, i.e. increasing the value of the asset, or is just keeping the asset in working order, which would be revenue expenditure (and therefore written off in the year in question).

For example, you have an existing asset, say a van. If parts wear out and you replace them you are not really adding value to the asset. In this instance, the accounting convention would require that the expenditure be written off against profits in the year that the cost was incurred. If, however, you put a new and more sophisticated engine in the van, which extends its life and improves its performance, this would probably increase its value. There will then be a good case for regarding the expenditure as Capex, and writing the cost of the new engine off, via depreciation, over the remaining life of the van. Frankly, capitalisation decisions similar to these are not based on very scientific criteria and management who make the final decisions can only be guided by the financial management and accounting conventions.

One problem that can arise here is that there can often be conflict between accountants and management. Management – certainly in times of making losses – will wish to capitalise as much expenditure as possible, the effect being to bolster the balance sheet and reduce losses. Accountants, on the other hand, may wish to apply the convention of conservatism and write off the expenditure as quickly as possible, thereby increasing losses. Obviously in times of high profits management may wish to apply the reverse decision.

WHY INVEST IN CAPEX?

Most businesses need assets to produce goods and services, such as machinery to manufacture goods for sale. The business you are in will determine what type of assets you will need. A firm of solicitors doesn't need the same investment in assets as a steel pipe manufacturer. However, even this is not as clear-cut as it looks, because sometimes decisions are taken based on desire rather than need, e.g. expensive cars, and others may treat assets simply as an investment, e.g. fine art. Decisions to invest in luxuries are not normally subject to the strict hurdles of investment criteria that we shall be discussing later, but are often the personal choice of individuals or management. The late Lord White of Hanson invested in racehorses, which apparently were corporate assets. Sometimes these decisions become a focus of conflict between levels of management, or between management and the workforce.

Over time, fixed assets need replacing, upgrading or augmenting due to a variety of reasons: expansion, old age, technical obsolescence, and so on.

Proposals for capital expenditure

Senior management will consider proposals for capital expenditure from managers responsible for various aspects of the business.

1 *Maintaining or increasing sales*

Capital expenditure to improve products or services, or expand products or services, for example buying new machinery or extra delivery vans. In this case the Capex proposal may well come from the marketing department. Most products or services have a limited lifespan in their original form. New ones have to be created and developed before the existing ones become obsolete. All expenditure here is charged to the development of the product or service and on a successful launch the total cost is capitalised, i.e. made an asset. Sometimes the new asset is registered as having a tradename, a trademark or a patent. These types of assets are called intangible assets for although you cannot touch them as you can machinery they do have a value, which reflects the cost of development. Consider the difficulty of trying to put a price on the brand name 'Coca-Cola' or 'Guinness', yet there is a clear value to those names. The professional accounting bodies have had difficulties in establishing fair valuations of tradenames etc. with companies who want to increase the value of intangible assets in their balance sheets, particularly when the decision is part of a defensive move against threatened takeover.

2 Maintaining or replacing premises and plant

New plant, equipment and buildings, or replacement of the same, are of course tangible assets and an accurate cost can go into the balance sheet. Decisions on what to build or purchase will involve professional people such as engineers, architects, etc. The accountant's role in such Capex decisions is to advise senior management on financing and depreciation policies.

3 Research and development

The expenditure on R & D (research and development) which, on any particular project, can include staff hours, equipment, rent and other overheads, can be capitalised and thus shown in the balance sheet. If the project is successful, leading to a new product, then the total costs can be calculated so as to establish the true investment in the new product. However, should the project prove to be unsuccessful – and therefore aborted – the whole cost of the project (assuming nothing is salvageable) will have to be written off to the profit and loss account in the year that the project was halted. Companies that invest heavily in R & D, for example drug firms and computer software development houses, will have enough historical information to estimate what proportion of their R & D projects will, on average, lead to proven products and will charge expenditure to their accounts accordingly.

4 *Exploration*

Exploration for such as oil, gas or minerals can also be regarded as capital expenditure, and when it leads to a 'find' then the total costs of exploring a particular field can be capitalised against the value of the reserves found. Unsuccessful exploration costs will be written off to the profit and loss account as and when the field is found to be 'dry'.

5 *Compliance*

Other forms of Capex may not necessarily improve the efficiency of an asset or prolong its life, but may be essential for reasons of compliance with Health and Safety legislation and/or pollution control. Here the return on the expenditure may well be below the company norms but clearly in these cases companies do not have a choice in the matter if they wish to continue in business.

CAPEX DECISIONS

The decision-making process regarding capital expenditure will depend upon the size and the control functions within the organisation. If you are a sole trader, Capex decisions are made by you, with or without taking advice. Large organisations inevitably lay down strict criteria for sanctioning Capex. An example of such criteria is as follows:

1   What is the total amount of money to be committed?

2   By what criteria (costing system) did we establish, or will we calculate, the total costs, so that the process by which we collect the costs can be verified?

3   Over what period of time (months/years) will the asset generate cash, through sales of products or services, and how long will the total cash recovery period be? (*This is known as the payback period: see chapter 16. When deciding what Capex proposals to invest in, the company will consider the length of payback periods of various proposals.*)

4   What is the average capital employed in the business and what return are we getting on that figure? (*See 'Return on Average Capital Employed' in chapter 8.*) How does this return compare with the Capex proposal under consideration? (*The UK's largest companies are demanding an average 15% return, with no proposal worse than 5%.*)

5   Are there any taxation benefits or development grants to be gained from this proposal? (*Governments encourage Capex in development areas by granting tax breaks, etc., so as to encourage investment and create employment.*)

6   What else could have been done with the money within the company? (*This is called 'opportunity cost'. In most larger organisations there is fierce competition for capital from other parts of the business. The opportunity cost is the value to the business of the project(s) that cannot be undertaken because of accepting this proposal.*)

7   How will the Capex be financed? (*Out of profits, bank loan, hire purchase, leasing, lease-back, raising money on the market?*)

8   What threats will the business meet by not investing in this Capex, i.e. will a competitor enter into the market to fill the product/service gap? (*If a competitor enters with up-to-date machinery that company will probably be able*

*to undercut your prices and take from you some of your
market share.)*

9 What is the life expectancy of the asset?

10 For production assets, what will be the level of availability? (*How often will it need to be shut down/refitted, etc.,
in the cycle of Planned Programmed Maintenance?*) What
will be the reliability? (*What is the risk that the availability will be lower than needed? New plant is reliable: it has
high availability; old plant is unreliable: it has low availability.*)

11 What are the repairs and maintenance costs to be incurred
over the life of the asset?

12 What are the political considerations? (*This is a very
important criterion for multinationals and their 'Rest of
the World' investment policies.*)

Once the relevant answers have been collected, a Capex
proposal can be drawn up for management. An example of
such a proposal is given in Figure 22.1.

Most companies have an administrative procedure for
capital expenditure proposals which will clearly define the
hurdles they will have to jump to be successful:

1 Generation of Capex proposals will be encouraged from
all divisions and departments of the organisation.

2 All Capex proposals will need to be written in a similar
format and be subject to the same criteria (offering a level
playing-field to those who must make the accept/reject
decisions between Capex proposals).

3 An independent management review (i.e. not from the
areas proposing the Capex investment, and often called a
Capex committee) will evaluate the cash outflows and
inflows of the proposals. Most companies acknowledge

Project Ajax

1. Proposal to build and commission a 30,000-tonnes polyresin plant at Ajax Industrial Site, Herts.

2. Assumptions:
   (a) All licences and permissions needed to operate the plant will be granted.
   (b) Sales per tonne of £10 are based on current market prices of £11.50 per tonne adjusted for min.-max price variation of the past three years. (Our estimate is a selling price below the current market price, to give a safety margin.)
   (c) Availability of plant once commissioned: 97.5% (We require it to be available this much of the year.)
   (d) Reliability of plant once commissioned: 96.7% (We expect this to be the actual reliability.)

3. Total cost of plant: £300,000.

4. Life expectancy at 100% production: 15 years. (Depreciation therefore £20,000 p.a.: £20,000 x 15 years' life expectancy).

5. Estimated net profit per annum: £54,000. (18% ROACE on £300,000 investment.)

Calculations (£'000)*

	Year 1				Year 2				Total
	qtr 1	qtr 2	qtr 3	qtr 4	qtr 1	qtr 2	qtr 3	qtr 4	
Cash outflows	50	70	80	60	10	10	10	10	300
Cash inflows	–	–	40	50	70	80	80	80	400
Monthly	(50)	(70)	(40)	(10)	60	70	70	70	
Cumulative	(50)	(120)	(160)	(170)	(110)	(40)	30	100	

Notes:

(1) Max cash exposure £170,000 (qtr 4, year 1)

(2) Payback by qtr 3 of year 2

(3) ROACE 18%

* For the sake of this example we have assumed cash inflows and outflows to demonstrate the layout of the calculation. Actual years would replace 'year 1' and 'year 2'.

Figure 22.1   *Capex proposal – an example*

that cashflow, not income, is the essential criterion.

4 The successful selection of proposals is based upon acceptance criteria already laid down, e.g. pay-back period and Return on Capital Employed.

5 Continual re-evaluation of investment projects after their acceptance.

TERMINOLOGY

A few expressions used in Capex proposals need specific explanation:

Net present value (NPV)

As discussed in chapter 16, this is an estimation of the value *today* of a payment that is to be made or received '*tomorrow*'. The payment is discounted by an amount that takes into account the time between now and the day that the payment is due. This amount is calculated having regard to expected interest rates and inflation. Pounds today are worth more than pounds tomorrow, because of these inflation uplifts and interest rates.

Inflation determines by how much sterling decreases in value and interest rates indicate how much we could earn on our money were we to invest it. Therefore all Capex project figures are adjusted to take into account the effects of inflation and interest rates.

The NPV of an investment project is the difference between the present value of the future revenues of the project and the present value of its future costs. If the return on the investment is calculated to be less than the return would be by investing the same amount of money elsewhere then the Capex proposal may be rejected unless there are other (political, health and safety, etc.) reasons for the investment.

Capital rationing

Capital rationing occurs at any time there is a budget constraint (a cap) on the amount of funds that can be invested during a specific period of time, e.g. a year. Such constraints are often used during a period of cash shortage and in particular in those companies that have a policy of financing all Capex from internal sources.

Capital risk

Capital risk considers the variability of possible returns. Risk is created by a wide variety of factors, some predictable and others more random, e.g. the economy in general, new technology, consumer preferences, labour conditions, political and environmental considerations, etc.

Financing Capex

The ideal method of raising or borrowing money should be appropriate to the appropriate assets. Short-term borrowings (overdrafts) should correctly be used to finance short-term working capital or short-term stock movements; conversely, long-term finance should be used to finance long-term capital expenditure (see chapter 17).

23

Parlez-vous Accountancy?

$\diamond$

A CCOUNTANCY is like a language: it sounds exotic to anyone who can't speak it. And, like any language when you do learn to speak it, you find the natives are talking about the same everyday, mundane things that we all talk about.

Accountancy is also a profession: it creates a mystique around itself to keep outsiders out and insiders in. The high priests are appointed 'Qualified Accountants' to relate the message to the populace. And to keep their exalted positions they maintain the mystique and incomprehensibility of the subject – mainly through the use of jargon and/or special language.

This A–Z of the most common terms won't make you an accountant, but it will break down the mystique, and translate the language so that you will be able to 'parlez accountancy' at the basic level. Page references will guide you to a fuller explanation of the more complex terms. Words in *italic* are the subject of their own entry.

Accruals
'Creditors' are liabilities which have not yet been paid but for which the company has received an invoice. There will also be some costs which have not been paid but which have also not yet been invoiced and these are 'accrued for', that is, they become 'accruals'. Basically, you take an educated guess at what bills are lurking round the corner, and an accrual represents the figure you've estimated.

Amortisation
See *Depreciation.*

Assets
See *Current assets* and *Fixed assets.*

Bad debt
When a company supplies goods or services on credit it creates *debtors*, i.e. people who owe it money. A debtor that is thought unlikely to pay, or cannot pay due to bankruptcy or liquidation, is called a bad debt. Bad debts are written off to the profit and loss account as a cost.

Balance sheet
The balance sheet is a 'snapshot photograph' at one point during the year, usually at the *year end*. It shows the assets owned by the company and the debts due by the company at that moment in time. It is the balance sheet which 'ties up' the accounts, as it summarises all the *double entry* book-keeping that goes on throughout the year (see chapter 6).

Book value
Generally speaking, assets are brought into the books (i.e. the books of accounts) at cost but *depreciation* is charged against the cost to reflect their diminution in value over time. At any given point, the asset is shown in the book therefore at an assumed value, known as book value.

Bought ledger / Bought day book
See *Purchases ledger / Purchases day book.*

Break-even
At that certain point of sales when all costs are covered, the company is at its break-even point. Any further activity then results in profit and any lesser activity results in a loss.

Budget
A budget is a proposal to spend or allocate resources up to a certain limit on certain items for a certain purpose within a certain period. In corporate terms the overall budget is divided between departments and each department has a budget-holder responsible for keeping to the plan (see chapter 15).

Capex
This is the abbreviation for capital expenditure which is discussed in chapter 22.

Capital
Capital is basically the financing of a company, i.e. the money which supports it. *Working capital* is essentially short-term; long-term capital would include *share capital*, long-term loans and the self-generated *profits* of the company.

Capital employed
This is another term for the long-term capital which supports the long-term assets of the company and is composed generally of *share capital*, share premium accounts, special reserves, long-term loans and accumulated *profits*.

Cash book
More properly, this should be called the 'bank book', as the cash book generally records transactions in and out of the main company bank account. Although cash books can be drawn up to deal with more than one bank account, it is common practice to have a particular cash book for each particular bank account, and it certainly makes transactions easier to record.

The key factor is that it reflects what is coming through the bank statements and enables a check between the company's records and the bank's records. This gives a third party confirmation of what the company believes is happening. It also serves to help the company keep an eye on the bank.

Cashflow

Cashflow is currently a buzzword, since people have (perhaps belatedly) recognised that it is cashflow, rather than *profit*, which keeps the company going. Maintaining cashflow means ensuring that money earned from sales is received and banked so that it is available to make purchases of other goods for resale or to pay overheads. Controlling cashflow is the key to short-term survival: a company must have the cash – or *current assets* such as short-term investments that it can quickly turn into cash – in order to pay its way day-to-day.

Charge: to 'take a charge over' ie a mortgage

When a body, for example a bank or lending institution gives a loan to a company it often requests, and takes, a charge over certain assets of that company. This means that it can take those assets in settlement of the debt if the debt is not repaid as agreed. The charge may be over specific assets, ie a building, a piece of machinery and so on or it may be over the general assets of the company in total.

Costs

'*Direct costs*' are those which can be directly attributed to production, for example materials, labour, production equipment. '*Indirect costs*' are those which relate to the running of the company but which are not necessarily related to the direct activity of selling. For example, the payroll costs of administration staff are a cost which have to be met regardless of the volume of sales activity. They must be brought into the calculation of costs to be covered but they are indirect in that they are not directly attributed to production.

Credit

(1) A period of credit is a period of deferred payment for purchases i.e. a period of delay between purchase and the payment for that transaction. The purchaser is the party which considers this period as credit; the seller considers it as

debt and considers the amount and the purchaser as *debtors*.
(2) A record in the *sales ledger* of a cash sale.

Creditors
(1) Creditors are bills still due to be paid by the company for
services or goods that have been supplied to it. See also
Debtors.
(2) People to whom a company owes money.

Current assets
Generally speaking, current assets includes stocks of items
for sale, *debtors*, short-term investments and money in the
bank. They are known as 'current' since they should be able
to be turned into cash for spending purposes within one year
(or more immediately if necessary).

They are also distinguished from *fixed assets* in that if they
are no longer held by the company, this doesn't destroy the
overall capacity of the business to continue; that is, the sale
of stocks can be replaced by other stocks, and further loans
can replace money lost, whereas if the fixed assets were to be
sold or lost, there would be nothing physical left (equipment,
buildings, etc) and the company could no longer carry on its
activities. The current assets are therefore an element of the
working capital, i.e. the money to run the business day-to-
day.

Current liabilities
Liabilities are, broadly speaking, various items which are
owed to other people such as balances owed to suppliers for
goods and services, and overdrafts which are, in effect,
money owed to the bank. Current liabilities relate to
payments due within a one-year period.

Debenture
A special form of loan, usually a bank loan, which is
supported by a document called a debenture which is a
charge over certain of, or all, the assets of the company.
Debentures are usually further supported by the periodic

presentation of figures to give comfort to the lender that the company is continuing to trade successfully and can support its loan.

Debtors
(1) Debtors are amounts owed to the company by people that it has sold to but who have not yet paid their bills. See also *Creditors*.
(2) People who owe the company money.

Depreciation
Because the company can't *write off* its *fixed assets* in one year – as they have a longer life – the accounts reflect the gradual 'wearing out' of fixed assets by apportioning a certain amount of the cost to each year of their life. This is shown in the profit and loss account as a cost known as depreciation, i.e. the annual cost of using the asset. If you pay £10,000 for a piece of equipment and it has a four-year life, then you would write off 25% of £10,000 each year. The same technique is applied to *leasing* except that is then known as 'amortisation'.

Discount
A discount is a reduction in price, usually offered as an incentive. A sales discount is a reduction in price to encourage customers to buy an item. A finance discount is a reduction in the amount we expect to receive for a sale, to encourage early or prompt payment.

Dividends
These are the shareholders' reward for their investment in the business, representing their '*interest*' on that investment.

Double-entry bookkeeping
Every transaction has two components: (1) we sell an item worth £10 and (2) someone pays us the £10. The basis of double-entry bookkeeping is that for every entry made in one part of the books (sales) there is a corresponding entry else-

where (income). (Every debit has a credit.) And because all
the entries have to be added together, so that in effect all the
pluses and the minuses cancel out, then the resulting
summary, known as the *balance sheet*, is so called because it
balances.

Equity
A common word used to describe shares. In legal terms, it
means to be equal.

Factoring
The outsourcing of debt collection to a factoring company
(p. 179–80).

Fixed assets
Fixed assets are those assets which are not used up immediately in producing sales, but which have a lifespan of at least
more than one year. Obvious examples would be buildings,
and the plant and equipment installed in them, which may
last for many years; and vehicles, which have a few years'
life.

Accountants don't *write off* the company's fixed assets
immediately in the *profit and loss account*, as an expense of
the year in which they are purchased, but rather they are
'written down' according to their *depreciation* over a predetermined number of years.

Fixed costs
Some costs don't vary in proportion to sales or manufacturing activity, for example, the rates on a building will not vary
whether one unit or a hundred units of a product are being
produced. These are known as fixed costs. In the *profit and
loss account* most of the overheads (that is, the expenses
deducted from gross profit, to leave net profit) are some form
of fixed cost and have to be incurred whatever the level of
activity undertaken.

Going concern
If a company is a 'going concern', this means it is healthy and able to continue into the foreseeable future, trading at a level sufficient to maintain its existence.

Goodwill
If somebody buys a business, they will pay a certain amount for the items they buy. These will include the *fixed assets* and also perhaps some *current assets* such as stocks of products, and so on. In fact, quite often a person will pay more for a company than the value of the items being purchased and this difference is known as goodwill. This is the reflection of the fact that the company is worth more than simply its physical assets because it has a good name and people will come and buy its goods because of that reputation.

Gross profit
Sales income, less the direct costs (see *Costs*) of making those sales, results in the gross profit.

Hedge
A company can buy commodities, products or money ahead of need, as a 'hedge' against future price changes. For example, a company which will need to pay some of its suppliers in dollars may buy dollars now, although it expects to actually use them in three months' time, if it believes that dollars will be more expensive in three months' time.

Historical cost
The principle of historical cost dictates that all entries in a set of company books should give the actual (historical) cost of purchase rather than, say, the cost of replacement at the present time.

HP (Hire Purchase)
In order to buy an asset over a period of time, perhaps five years, it is possible to arrange finance so that possession of the asset can be taken immediately but payment made for it

over an extended period of time. The price for this is an interest charge paid, also over the period of time. Actual ownership of the asset is reserved until a proportion of the payment has been made.

Interest
This amounts to the cost of money over time. If you take a loan, you will be expected to repay more than just the amount of that loan. The additional amount, called interest, gives the lender a profit on the transaction, and also reflects the fact that in times of inflation money in the future is worth less than money today.

Journal entries
When an item has been wrongly 'posted' into the books, or for some reason an item has to be 'reposted' to another place in the books, a journal entry is a way of taking a sum from one nominal ledger, or other ledger account, and placing it in another such account. Each journal entry must have a balancing total of debits and credits to maintain the double entry system.

Leasing
Some companies may choose not to own their assets but rather to lease them (i.e. rent them) over a period of time. The asset does not become the company's legal possession but the lease payment entitles them to a use of the asset within certain conditions and for a certain period of time.

Liquidity
Liquidity refers to the amount of cash, or *assets* easily convertible into cash, available to a company.

Net profit
After *gross profit* has been established by deducting costs from sales income, there are a number of ongoing costs of

running the company which have to be met and after these have been deducted the company is left with a net profit (or loss).

Nominal ledger

Just as the *sales ledger* deals with sales, and the *purchases ledger* (bought ledger) deals with purchases, so the nominal ledger deals with all the other expenses incurred by the company, such as salaries, heat, light, telephone, and so on. The nominal ledger is therefore a summary of those individual costs under their individual headings.

Overdraft

A form of short-term bank funding whereby the bank agrees to allow you to spend more than you have in your account up to a fixed limit in return for an overdraft fee and *interest*. Overdrafts are legally repayable on demand.

Overtrading

See *Working capital*.

Payments in advance

In the *profit and loss account*, in order that expenses relate to the same period as income, expenditure within the year has to be 'isolated' to that year. It may be that one month prior to the *year end* an insurance premium is paid for the year ahead but, since this would relate to eleven months of the next year, only one month can be carried into the year in which payment was made against sales of that year. The remaining eleven months are a payment in advance against the next year.

Petty cash book

This is the book recording cash transactions in the company. Most commonly what is known as an 'imprest' system is used, whereby a specific float is given to a department which then has to record what it does with its cash money in the petty cash book. A float of, say, £100 may be given to a department and over the course of a month £89 may be spent on various items which will be recorded in the petty cash book; a cheque drawn from the bank to the value of £89 will then bring the float up to £100 again for the ensuing month.

Prior year adjustments
This phrase relates to adjustments in a set of accounts where figures for the previous years need to be amended. Prior year adjustments are used to correct fundamental errors of previous years or to reflect a change in accounting policy (such as a rate of *depreciation*).

Profit
By the time the mystical language of accountancy has confused the issue, even a definition of profit can seem uncertain. It is, however, very simple: it is the excess of money made by selling something, above the costs of buying or producing it in the first place. See *Gross profit*, *Net profit*, *Retained profits*.

Cynical critics of accountancy will tell you that an accountant can produce any profit you want. There is a joke about the company director interviewing accountants who asks the first candidate 'What is 1 + 1?' but rejects that candidate when he replies '2'. The second applicant also replies '2' and is rejected. The successful candidate is the one who replies 'What do you want it to be?'

Profit and loss account
This is a summary of the income earned during a period (usually a year) and the expenses needed to earn that income.

Provision
Where a cost cannot be quantified or is not known for certain, a provision (an estimated amount) can be added to costs in the *profit and loss account* and simultaneously added to *creditors* in the *balance sheet*. The actual payment, when-

ever it is made, is set against the provision and the difference adjusted in a subsequent profit and loss account.

Purchases ledger / Purchases day book

Purchases of goods for resale – or materials for manufacture into goods for resale – are recorded through a special purchases system which has entries in both the purchases day book and the purchases ledger.

The ledger contains a summary of the purchases from each individual supplier (and a further entry is made from the *cash book* when that supplier is paid). At any given moment the individual supplier's page in the ledger will show the total amount of purchases from that supplier, the total amount of money paid to them and the balance owed.

The day book records invoices received from suppliers as and when they are received so that there is a total cost from suppliers for a given period, irrespective of where the supplies come from. Automatically, therefore, our purchases have been broken down into time (the period of purchases) and type (who the items are purchased from).

Also known as the *bought ledger* and *bought day book.*

Refinancing

The repaying of debts by taking out new debts. This will often happen when interest rates have changed. Householders commonly refinance their most major debt, their mortgage, by taking out a new lower-interest mortgage to pay off an old one.

Replacement cost

Although assets are traditionally shown in the *balance sheet* at *historical cost* (their cost price when purchased), a company is wise to be aware of the replacement cost of its assets (their price at the present time).

Retained profits

That part of the profit remaining after taxation and dividends have been paid. This is the profit available to put back into the business.

Sales ledger / Sales day book

This is exactly the same as for the *purchase ledger* and *purchase day book* except that here we are dealing with our sales rather than purchases. The sales ledger records sales to our various customers, amounts received from them and the amounts due from them at any given time. The sales day books record the amount sold each day.

Security

This is an *asset* pledged against a loan. If the loan is not repaid then the asset is taken away and sold by the lender to recover their loan.

Share capital

Companies are owned by a group of people, each of whom has a number of shares, reflecting how much of the company they own. Somebody with 50% of all the shares, for example, owns half of the company. Share capital is therefore their stake in the company.

Shares give the owner certain rights: to receive dividends and to appoint the people who run the company. Interestingly, they don't give owners the right to manage the company – the board of directors is appointed for this. (In smaller companies the shareholders and the board of directors may be the same people but in larger companies this is rarely the case.) (p. 49.)

Solvency

A company is solvent when it can pay its debts on a day-to-day basis and is insolvent when it cannot. Solvency is therefore a measure of the company's short-term financial health.

Spreadsheets

A spreadsheet is simply a summary form, presenting any one of a multitude of situations. One type of spreadsheet is the *cashflow* summary, showing income and outgoings on a month-by-month basis, building up across the page towards the whole year; another, on a similar format, shows profit forecasts for a whole year.

There is a special spreadsheet known as the 'extended trial balance' which enables the entries in the *purchase ledger, sales ledger* and *nominal ledger*, together with *journal entries, cash book* and *petty cash* entries, all to be summarised on one page. This then produces a draft set of *profit and loss account* and *balance sheet* figures for preparation into final accounts.

Computerised spreadsheets have a facility whereby if any one figure is changed, the computer will automatically work through the rest of the figures, confirming or changing each one, to bring the whole spreadsheet back into arithmetical accuracy.

Trading profit
Gross profit in a trading company.

Treasury department
The department in a company which deals with the *cash books*, bank reconciliations and the management of deposits and expenditure.

Turnover
Turnover means total sales income during a period and comes from the expression 'stock turn', that is, the amount of times that the average stock of the company is 'turned over' (sold) during a period.

Unsecured
If a loan is given to a company without *security* then the loan is said to be 'unsecured'. This means that if the loan is not repaid, there are no specific assets which can be taken away by the lender to be sold to recover the money. In the case of a *liquidation*, unsecured loans will only be repaid to the extent that there are funds available, after paying off any secured or preferred loans.

Variable costs
These occur generally in the build-up to *gross profit* and are costs which vary directly in proportion to the activity level of sales or manufacture. For example, if you are going to double the level of your sales, you will have to double the level of your purchases (of materials or finished goods) in order to meet those sales.

Venture capital
A specialised form of company funding, provided by venture capital firms. Here, funds are made available to companies wishing to expand in cases where – because of perceived risks – the proposals are not attractive to banks or other lenders (p. 183).

Working capital
Working capital is basically the *current assets* less the *current liabilities*: it is the net current assets available for day-to-day running of the business. When working capital dries up, meaning there is no cash available to purchase the goods necessary to make future sales, then the company may be guilty of 'overtrading', i.e. it is obtaining orders successfully, but is no longer able to meet the demand that it is generating.

Write down
The estimation of the diminution in value of an asset charged as a cost.

Write off
(See *Depreciation*)

About the Authors

John Spencer, FCA
John Spencer is Managing Partner of Connor, Spencer & Co., Chartered Accountants. As director of APW Training, he works as a specialist trainer and lecturer in Management Development Skills, and specialist lecturer in Accountancy, Finance and Taxation. He is also a consultant to the Financial Services sector. His list of clients include companies in the entertainment and media industries, as well as in the industrial and commercial fields. He is well known as a contributor to magazines, radio and television on a variety of 'personal development' subjects. He is author of many business books, including *How to Get the Most out of Your Accountant*, and *Getting Paid*; and co-author, with Adrian Pruss, of *Managing Your Team* and *How to Implement Change in Your Company*.

Adrian Pruss, BA, ACIS, MIMgt
Adrian Pruss is a city-trained accountant. He is Senior Partner of APW Consultancy, and a director of APW Training. Before founding APW, he held various academic and boardroom positions. He is a Management Consultant specialising in organisational review, cost reduction, and change programmes; he is also a Management Development consultant and trainer for multinationals, industrial and commercial organisations in Europe, the USA and Africa. With John Spencer, he is co-author of *Managing Your Team*, and *How to Implement Change in Your Company*.

For details of finance courses based on this book, and other training programmes, contact:

APW Training

at:

2c Leyton Road
Harpenden
Herts, AL5 2TL
Telephone: 01582 468592

Fax: 01582 461979

e-mail: jspencer@dial.pipex.com

Index

MANAGEMENT BOOKS FROM THE SAME AUTHORS

How to Implement Change In Your Company: So everyone's happy with the result

Change is an exciting experience, one that is highly motivational if presented in the right manner. This book is packed with positive and practical advice which will help you to introduce change and see it as a necessary part of your company's growth.

hardback £22.50
paperback: £9.99

Managing Your Team: How to organise people for maximum results

The ability to build and lead a team is a vital management skill. In *Managing Your Team* you will learn how to create and runs teams and departments that will achieve high levels of commitment, performance and effectiveness.

paperback: £8.99

Both of these titles are published by **Piatkus.**
For a free brochure with further information on our full range of titles, please write to:

Piatkus Books
FREEPOST 7 (WD4505)
London W1E 4EZ

PIATKUS